I'm Right
—You're Wrong

Think Better, Argue Better, and Stop Lying to Yourself.

SIA MOHAJER

Contents

Dear Reader,

Before we start this journey.

I'm Sia Mohajer, and I write science-based articles explaining the psychology, habits, and routines that create successful business and life. I have been doing this for fifteen years and I don't plan to stop anytime soon.

I <u>greatly</u> appreciate you reading this book and your interest in my work is <u>extremely</u> important to me.

On my personal website, I research and write weekly articles about business, life and personal development. The question that I strive to ask is, "<u>How can I improve my life every day</u>".

If science-based self-improvement is something you are interested in, please sign up to my weekly newsletter – where I will send you <u>free books</u> and articles. (Sign up by clicking on this text.)

If weekly emails bother you or you simply aren't interested, no problem – please <u>don't</u> sign up.

I still like you for reading this book and hope you enjoy it.

Sincerely,

Sia M.

Chapter 1:
It All Starts with a Story

♦ ♦ ♦

The day after the space-shuttle Challenger disaster, Professor Ulric Neisser had his students write down precisely where they were when they heard the news of this explosion.[i] He asked them to provide specific details about their experience: how they felt, what they saw, and where they were. Two-and-a-half years later, he asked them for the same information. While fewer than one in ten got the details right, almost all of them were certain their memories were accurate. Even when they were shown their original writings, over half of them refused to change their minds; they denied reality to maintain their beliefs in their current opinions.

This experiment became widely cited; one neurologist, Robert Burton, viewed Neisser's Challenger study as emblematic of an essential quality of the human mind. In his book, *On Being Certain*, Burton argues that "certainty" is a mental state; it is a feeling like anger or pride that can help guide us in our decision-making. However, this feeling of certainty isn't dependent on objective truth—it rises out of involuntary brain mechanisms similar to feelings of love and anger; they function independently of

1

reason. Your feelings of certainty have absolutely nothing to do with how correct you are. We are all quite skilled at believing whatever we want. Our thinking is distorted by cognitive errors; these are ways that the mind convinces us of something that really isn't true. Like believing in the boogie man when you were ten year old, we can find evidence of our beliefs, even when they don't exist. Cognitive errors demonstrate the myriad of ways your brain attempts to hold together a meaningful worldview by trying to win arguments and persuade others they are wrong.

This "feeling of knowing" has some evolutionary benefits. Being absolutely certain and possessing a strong level of conviction keeps us confident and allows us to complete tasks we might otherwise avoid. Raising confident children is a hallmark of good parenting. One of parents' primary roles is to build up children's confidence and make them believe they are capable and worthy. Since the time our parents congratulated us for tieing our shoelaces and using the bathroom by ourselves, our self-confidence has been artificially built up. We feel certain in our abilities and each challenge is approached through parentally-reinforced stepping stones. Parents encourage us even when we aren't capable, or smart or talented. The problem is this falsely-bestowed confidence often carries on into adulthood, making us confident fools. We become ignorant of our own inability and lack of knowledge. In psychology, this widely demonstrated and researched error is called the Dunning Kruger bias, named after renowned psychologists Justin Kruger and David Dunning. The **Dunning–Kruger effect** is a cognitive bias wherein relatively unskilled individuals suffer from illusory superiority, mistakenly assessing their ability to be much higher than is accurate. Feeling certain is a trademark of this confident tomfoolery. Certainty makes us feel good; we don't like the "jerk" who comes in and spoils all our ignorant fun. Or, as Donald Trumph once said, "My IQ is one of the highest – and you all know it!".

Burton describes our insistence of being right as a mental equivalent of physical addiction. He states that many people, "derive more pleasure from final answers than ongoing questions, and want definite one-stop shopping solutions to complex social problems and unambiguous endings to movies and novels".[ii] The pleasure we derive from our "feelings of knowing" manifests itself mostly as pride and ignorance. However, the difference between supposed certitude and reality can have serious moral consequences. Think about making an important life decision, how extensively do we examine our own decisions making process? We generally ask questions and look for appropriate answers; however, the problem with such an approach is that our answers are often self-supporting and unexamined. We make decisions based on answers to questions that already skew our focus. We feel certain that our questions are the right ones to be asking and therefore, avoid reflecting on the questions themselves.

I mention the above examples for several reasons. First, the majority of people dislike being wrong. This is especially true in social situations and in contexts where "being wrong" jeopardizes an idea or opinion that has become a part of our identity. Second, we avoid reflecting on and understanding our own biases—even when presented with contradictory evidence. Finally (and most importantly), we often feel the need to defend our ideas to the death—rather than admitting we're wrong. In practice, this leads to bad communication, resentments, and failed relationships.

The Internet is full of arguments. Go on any message

board and you'll discover a microcosm of ignorance. Full-grown adults will debate who has "less of a life" on online video game messaging systems; they will go into "cyber-rage" over the ethical considerations of religion vs. atheism. The online world is rife with man's innate need to start conflicts with others. The term "Internet Troll" describes individuals who enjoy starting arguments and upsetting people by posting inflammatory, shocking, or off-topic comments on online forums with hopes of disturbing these communities and provoking them to argument. "Trolls" have become part of the regular Internet landscape. We might speculate on their identities, but we will probably never know if a troll is a twelve-year old boy at his grandmother's computer or a 45-year old unemployed man sitting at home. In reality, it doesn't matter. Trolls represent something that exists within all of us; our innate need to <u>be right</u>.

If I presented you with valid information and recommended a change in your thinking or lifestyle, how would you react?

Try This Exercise:

Give someone some unsolicited advice. Even if you offer them absolutely terrific advice, they probably won't accept it. People generally listen to our advice, nod with a perfunctory smile, and carry on as they were.

Typically, we humans only allow outside advice to "sink in" when life forces us to change our perspectives; even then, we often take credit for others' ideas. This is the logic behind an intervention; addicts are literally forced to listen to their friends' advice—and most of the time it doesn't help them at all. We are stubborn creatures. However, this isn't our fault—we were born this way.

We aren't born to learn from every situation. We aren't programmed to seek the truth. We haven't evolved to use reason. We are programmed to make our worlds as simple as possible. Simplicity means creating rules and applying those rules everywhere. These rules, called heuristics, are cognitive "rules of thumb". We apply these general rules to all stimuli; this allows us to rapidly evaluate and categorize the massive amount of information, people, and events in our daily experience. Heuristics allow our brains to take in an almost infinite amount of information, process it, and provide us with a stream of consciousness for understanding our world.

Our brain is our accountant; it "does the math for us". Do you want to bother with an endless list of numbers, graphs, and equations - or would you prefer a well-organized summary? Our "mental accountant" provides this essential service; however, just like any accounting whiz, it sometimes makes bad assumptions. These errors rear their ugly heads as cognitive biases and logical errors that make us susceptible to mistakes.

We often demonize these errors in thinking and shame those who stereotype others. While some people openly display their cognitive errors and biases, others stand behind a veil of contradictions and place blame—all the while unaware of their own stereotypes. As long as we have human brains, this world will never be rid of biases, stereotypes, or "groupthink". Unless we develop a cybernetic brain that annexes those regions responsible for evolutionary-based survival-oriented decision-making, a remedy for this problem doesn't seem to be anywhere in sight.

At this point you may be thinking, "How can I overcome this and think more rationally and effectively? There must be an answer."

There is. We call it "reasoning".

Reasoning is generally seen as a means of improving our knowledge and making better decisions. However, evidence shows that the types of reasoning we most commonly use often lead to poor decisions. While we may think we're conducting our lives in a "reasonable" fashion, the research shows otherwise.[iii] Abundant research has helped compile a list of over thirty cognitive biases that we engage in regularly. Perhaps we should rethink the function of reason; it may not be to provide clarity, but rather to serve another purpose— more effective arguments with others. Our human ability to reason developed out of a need to devise arguments to persuade others—and evaluate the arguments of our peers. Reasoning of this nature is very flexible, due to our massive dependence on communication and our vulnerability to misinformation.

A growing body of evidence in modern psychology and neuroscience shows that we can better understand our decision-making ability through the context of this hypothesis. Most notably, our performance on standard reasoning tasks is quite poor when compared to our performance in As New York Times bestselling author Chris Mooney stated in a recent article, "Poor performance in standard reasoning tasks is explained by the lack of argumentative context. When the same problems are placed in a proper argumentative setting, people turn out to be skilled arguers. Skilled arguers, however, are not after the truth but after arguments supporting their views."[iv] In other words, when we are given sides to identify with, we become skilled arguers. We are certain in our convictions and absolutely sure the other side is wrong (or more biased than we are). We use our reasoning abilities to prove our arguments' superiority while demolishing and rejecting opposing arguments.

This is a pretty radical departure from the classic "Cartesian" view of reasoning (developed by Rene Descartes). The idea is simple: we reason to critically examine our beliefs. We discard "wrong" beliefs and create more reliable ones which help us to better understand the world. The understanding we gain in this way is supposed to help us make better decisions. The problem with this classical view of reasoning is that it's hard to reconcile with a plethora of modern psychological evidence. Since the early 1970s, notable researchers (Amos Tversky and Daniel Kahneman) have systematically demonstrated the numerous failures of our decision-making processes. Their research has shown that we are not only prone to a multitude of errors; we also have an uncanny ability to deceive ourselves, maintain wholly-fictitious beliefs, create biased realities, and justify any actions we take.[v] These new scientific findings disagree with the Cartesian model of reasoning.

We Learned to Argue to Fight

The argumentative theory of reasoning proposed by Dan Sperber theorizes a very different function. Sperber believes that reasoning exists to fulfill the social function of finding reasons to argue with others and persuade them to agree with us.

Sperber's theory is backed by evolutionary rationale. Argumentative theory holds that communication plays a crucial role in human activities—and we evolved to master it. The collaborative activities of hunting, gathering, fighting, and raising children required us to evaluate information as trustworthy or unreliable—to distinguish valid information from potentially-dangerous inaccurate information. Our need to evaluation information made us sensitive to lies and deception; we developed listening mechanisms to better analyze information. Think of this as an ancient "bullshit detection system".

One method our ancestors used to improve their communication as speakers and listeners was argument. The speaker provided reasons that supported a certain conclusion; listeners evaluated these reasons and decided whether or not they would accepted the speaker's conclusion. People playing both of these roles used listening and speaking reasoning to evaluate information for lies, deception, inaccuracies or to further enhance their persuasive skills. If this reasoning was successful, human communication was improved.

A solid conclusion is supported by good arguments. The resulting acceptance benefits both sides—the speaker who convinced the listener and the listener who acquired a valuable piece of information. If this seems too convoluted, just think of reasoning as a "bullshit detection system" that naturally activates when we are skeptical about something.

This evolutionary-based approach is consistent with our current knowledge of human cognition. This view is also referred to as the "Social Brain Hypothesis" or the "Machiavellian Intelligence Hypothesis". Both of these hypotheses state that most human cognition evolved to match the demands of our social world. In this social world, arguing with others, detecting bullshit, and being stubborn are all top-of-the-list attributes. Because this is a book about arguments, and not human cognition theories, I wouldn't describe this in any more detail. Just keep in mind that the evolution of reason occurred not to find truth, but to win.

I'm Right—You're Wrong.

Our biases and deficits in reasoning all stem from one key source: the automatic processes that simplify our world. Numbers expose the most obvious deficits in our reasoning skills, especially numbers involving probabilities. We have a hard time judging probability without referring to past events. This best example of this is known as the gambler's fallacy. The gambler's fallacy, also known as the Monte Carlo fallacy, is the mistaken belief that, if something happens more frequently than normal during some period, it will happen less frequently in the future, or that, if something happens less frequently than normal during some period, it will happen more frequently in the future. Our brains are powerful engines of decision making, but probabilities throw a wrench in our cognitive gears. The reason is simple – for most of our evolutionary history, we didn't have to think about probabilities. We existed in much simpler times. We followed much simpler equations like this: BEAR = "run as fast as humanly possible".

Modern society has inundated us with choice—to the point of paralysis. We take events that are statistically highly unlikely and elevate them into the realm of possibility. You might get eaten by a shark while you're swimming at the beach but it's <u>extremely unlikely</u>. You might win the lottery but <u>you probably won't</u>. When humans look at complex situations, we look for a way to understand them. We apply the same simple "bear-equals-run-away" formulas to modern problems and ideas—the result is a mismatched response.

This mismatched response is especially obvious when our emotions are evoked. When we feel fearful or anxious about an event, we assume it is more likely to occur. Do you know anyone who keeps a loaded weapon in their house in fear of a potential attack? The probability of such an event occurring is low; the chances of your average American needing to fight off "bad guys" in the middle of the night are actually lower than being struck by lightning.[vi] When analyzed rationally, we can see that people are statistically more likely shoot themselves or their family with their weapon than ward off a criminal.[vii] Unfortunately, none of this will change the average person's mind; owning a gun provides a sense of safety, even though this is "safety" against something that will almost certainly never happen.

The issue of safety is a huge aspect of the "War on Terror". This war is not new; from 1975 to 2003, the U.S. spent 1.3 trillion[viii] fighting terrorism—over 90$ million for each person killed. Terrorism is an awful thing and I agree we must defend ourselves; however, these expenditures aren't justified in a country that faces a host of socioeconomic problems. Our response to terrorism and violence demonstrates this point: when we are afraid, our rational logic is overwhelmed and we improperly weigh the pros and cons of our decisions.

You Are Always Right

The first rule of any argument is this: <u>you are always right</u>. (You just need the other person to acknowledge this.) It can be frustrating when others don't agree your argument is superior to theirs. We may eventually give up and tell ourselves (in a self-congratulatory way) they "just aren't on our level" or "simply aren't mature enough to get it". When others don't recognize our "impeccable" logic and "solid" conclusions, we inevitably come to one conclusion – they are biased and can't think clearly. At this point, most arguments quickly degenerate into blame and anger.

No one wants to be accused of being "biased". In our politically-correct society of moral and ethical fairness, being "biased" is like being possessed by a demonic entity. People who make biased decisions and judgments aren't evil characters with agenda of manipulation and deception; rather, they suffer from the same systematic distortions of reality as all humans. When presented with others' opinions (which we view as biased), we may think, "Why would they spread these lies" or "Why would they believe this?" We commonly believe others' agendas differ from our own. Our human brains ignore flaws in arguments we agree with and find the flaws in those we don't. We want to win more than we want to seek the truth.

It's extremely important to us to live in a world where we are right. We are taught from childhood to believe in ourselves and not be influenced by others. This resilience is described best in what psychologists call "Self-Perception Theory". In all realms of social science, self-perception theory helps determine, modify and regulate our future actions and behaviors.

It goes a little something like this: "I see myself as a kind and generous person. I embody these values and my actions should reflect them." If I were to engage in an action that contradicted this self-image I would feel, what psychologists call – cognitive dissonance. Loosely defined as "feeling bad". The result of this dissonance may range from guilt to a power need to justify your actions.

Our actions follow in line with our values; we conform to whatever value systems we subscribe to. The method of "change the values – change the behaviors" is used in most forms of propaganda; attacking and manipulating people's value systems causes systemic changes in their behavior. What we value dictates the actions we feel we should or shouldn't engage in.

If we violate our values, we are faced with two choices—both equally undesirable: First, we can feel cognitive dissonance (guilt, anxiety, stress, disappointment, etc.) at our failure to live in accordance with our higher values. Second, we can reframe our actions to suit our value systems by manipulating their contexts, meanings, and intentions. Both of these methods end with the same result—conformity to values.

You may be thinking, "What do values and behavior have to do with errors in logic?"

We not only think others are more biased than we are, we also believe ourselves immune from bias. We are not an "average" person, we are an "enhanced", "better" type of human. We feel that our arguments enjoy a sense of logic and reason above that of other people. We are not seeking truth—we want to win. One of the best ways to win is to always see ourselves as winners—even if we have to tilt the odds in our favor. We don't have to know what we are talking about, we just need an opinion – regardless of how ignorant it is.

This idea was demonstrated by Cornell University psychologists David Dunning and Justin Kruger. In a recent article Dunning explains how he explains, "In our work, we ask survey respondents if they are familiar with certain technical concepts from physics, biology, politics, and geography. A fair number claim familiarity with genuine terms like *centripetal force* and *photon*. But interestingly, they also claim some familiarity with concepts that are entirely made up, such as the *plates of parallax*, *ultra-lipid*, and *cholarine*. In one study, roughly 90 percent claimed some knowledge of at least one of the nine fictitious concepts we asked them about. In fact, the more knowledgeable respondents considered themselves in a general topic, the more familiarity they claimed with the meaningless terms associated with it in the survey."[ix]

Unskilled people often believe they are more skilled, knowledgeable, or experienced than they actually are. Ironically, highly-skilled people often underestimate their relative abilities; they often think tasks which are easy for them are just as easy for others. In other words, we often think we're better at things than we are—in actuality, we're just overconfident. We use this same confidence to mask our ignorance and incompetence.

People who suffer from this bias in the extreme are unable to accept that they're wrong. This is a puzzling idea: once a person's ignorance is exposed, doesn't honesty take its place? This is rarely the case; most people will just "dig in" and defend their potentially-ridiculous points of view. In a recent article, Dunning explained, "What's curious is that, in many cases, incompetence does not leave people disoriented, perplexed, or cautious. Instead, the incompetent are often blessed with an inappropriate confidence, buoyed by something that feels to them like knowledge."[x]

Unfortunately, our perceptions of our abilities and those of others are not based on solid evidence; we are prone to making assumptions and indulging in "wishful thinking". Rational thought takes deliberate effort and time. Our reality and our perception of it can function independently of each other. People often chose to live in a fictional world and only face reality when they must. Dunning [xi] described this condition as "the anosognosia of everyday life". Anosognosia is a physical disability (typically caused by brain injuries) in which patients deny or are totally unaware of the existence of a disability.

The Dunning-Kruger Bias is a radical example that shows how deeply entrenched our "need to be right" is in our psyches. Even in the face of massive contradiction, we are often unable to face our double-standards. The need to "feel right" is biologically programmed into us to such a degree that we are willing to forgo the truth to support our opinions and ideas. Even when faced with clear evidence of our bad decisions, we will still stubbornly side with the opinions and ideas we identify with.

However, we all differ in our eagerness to be "certain". Research has shown that we have a genetic basis for seeking certainty.[xii] A gene associated with risk-tasking and novelty-seeking makes some people more prone to striving for certainty and safety than others. This idea proposes an interesting question: "Do people get different degrees of pleasure from the "feeling of knowing?"

Not only is there a genetic component to our need to feel the pleasure of certainty, there are strong brain-reward systems that make this "feeling of knowing" essential to our learning processes.

How do you feel when you finish reading a book? How do you feel when you finally solve a difficult problem that has bothered you for a long time?

We get a strong sense of satisfaction from gaining new knowledge. However, there is a slightly less tangible feeling within that basic satisfaction—a kind of smug happiness about the knowledge we possess. Just like people who collect cars, trophies, or accomplishments we enjoy "collecting" knowledge. The key component of our brain-reward circuitry is our mesolimbic dopamine system[xiii]. This system is a set of nerve cells that originates in the upper-brain stem. Our feelings of certainty are rewarded by "feel-good hormones"—primarily dopamine and serotonin. When we engage in argument, our words fight a metaphorical battle; if we are triumphant, our brains flood with these hormones. Adrenaline and dopamine make us feel amazing, dominant—and even invincible.

So, If we feel this good when we're acknowledged as "right" – how about when we are perceived as "wrong"?

We Are What We Are Taught

From a young age, we are taught to feel shame. Shame for deeds that harm others or don't comply with social norms. Our teachers, parents and friends use shame to make us conform to societal expectations. The experience is often so traumatizing that it serves to self-regulate future behavior. In his book, "Shame and Psychotherapy", Dr. Marc Miller states, "Shame is often experienced as the inner, critical voice that judges whatever we do as wrong, inferior, or worthless." [xiv] Shame is often associated with being wrong. While we enjoy being right, we hate being wrong. Shame is even more excruciating when we feel it in public (rather than private) settings; the more people involved, the greater our sense of shame. This is why yelling at your child in public is so terribly effective.

Before you start thinking that shame is some "evil enemy", please consider the important role it plays. It is normal to feel shame about ourselves and our behaviors—it isn't a symptom of illness. If we didn't experience shame, we'd be abnormal—and face a serious risk of psychopathy. Shame (and its good friend, Mr. Guilt) help us recognize our mistakes and (hopefully) rectify them. This idea (that shame and guilt serve important regulating functions, help us examine our behaviors, and allow us to use reason to improve them) seems like a great theory. However, there's a problem with this: as I said earlier, our reasoning didn't evolve to make us better thinkers, it evolved for one simple reason—to make sure that we <u>win</u>.

When it comes to our own mistakes, we don't want to feel shame and guilt. We just want to "be understood" or justify our reasoning. We reserve critical judgment for others—not ourselves. We are keenly aware of our own internal states; however, other people's feeling exist only in the world of our supposition and assumption.

We use our "need to be right", our biases, and our cognitive manipulations to maintain our worldviews. In our attempts to prove others wrong and destroy their arguments, we engage in many flawed tactics. We establish premises and make assumptions that serve to further our points while dismantling our opponents' positions. Our positions are often logical fallacies and derive from one origin: our need to be right and convince others of our infallibility.

Our arguments are typically "chock full" of logical errors. As you progress through this book and explore the various types of "errors in argument", you will appreciate one overwhelming fact: you are guilty of almost all of these. Look around you: people so often commit horrendous errors in logic and make decisions based on invalid premises. Intelligence is no help in this; smart people are just as susceptible to these "errors in argument" as any others.

People who can identify others' logical fallacies and avoid them in their own arguments are exceedingly valuable and rare. In a world in which we are bombarded with information of all kinds, we rely on our automatic systems of evaluation and categorization to do the "mental accounting" of life. However, these mental shortcuts often lead us into fallacious reasoning—they keep us from knowing the truth. Our inability to think critically makes us vulnerable to manipulation by those skilled in the arts of rhetoric.

By looking at how terrible our arguments truly are, we can gain a sense of clarity. You can transform yourself through a process of self-examination. How do you defend certain ideas and need to "feel right" in your communications with others? Clear thinking is more important than your egotistical ambitions to be "more right" than others and feel superior to them. Clear thinking is "ideal reason"—reasoning that makes your life better and increases the quality of your decisions. Contrast this with your biological imperative to maintain a sense of "certainty". Do you want to continue down an energy-intensive path of deceiving yourself? Or, do you want to re-examine your "need to be certain" in the context of logical fallacies and create a path to clearer thinking?

The Ancient Greeks viewed reason as a higher characteristic than all others. Reason was considered the duty of all civilized men. They believed that reason was something humans shared with nature itself, a link between human fallibility and the divine order of the cosmos itself. Within this mind-and-soul symbiosis the Greeks called "Psyche", Plato described reason as a natural monarch which should rule other the other parts of us (such as spirit and emotion). Plato described the highest potential for human happiness and well-being as existing within a life that is consistently, excellently, and completely in according with reason.[xv]

In the subsequent sections, you will be given opportunities to take back your logical faculties from your need to be "certain". As I detail the various logical errors humans make, you will begin to realize how often you employ these in your arguments and discussions— and how often you accept them in others. You have probably not been trained in the art of clear thinking— within this lies a dangerous potential. People with superior persuasion skills may trick you into accepting ideas you might not otherwise choose. Learning to see your cognitive errors will strengthen you and help you defend yourself from the dangers of easy social compliance.

Just One More Thing

I must say this before we start—people don't like to be told they're wrong. This chapter is a clear testament to that fact. Your attempts to convince your fellow human beings of their errors may prove difficult. Telling someone their opinions and supporting logical arguments are full mistakes is a good way to pick a fight.

Try this exercise: Tell someone that they are wrong in real life and watch their face turn red.

When logic fails, a more primal need to prove yourself manifests – one that isn't scared to attack. Not only are people <u>unwilling</u> to budge positions they've held for years—they're almost totally <u>unable</u> to do so. When challenged, people doesn't typically re-examine their beliefs; instead, they often entrench themselves deeper and defend their ideas.

When you identify with an idea long enough, it becomes a part of you. We defend these internalized ideas as if we are being physically attacked.

So, tread lightly. This may make the title of the book

sound like a complete misnomer, but it isn't. By understanding how logical errors work, you can help others see the same mistakes in themselves that you have discovered in yourself. Just don't expect them to listen to you. Worse yet—they may attack you.

As I explain the various logical fallacies, please do a few things. Think of this text as a workbook—a workbook of self-reflection. As we discuss each fallacy, think about the last time you committed this particular "fault in logic". At the time, did you know your logic was incorrect or incomplete? Reflect on yourself as you read—and reap the rewards of a clearer mind.

> *Humans are creatures who spend their lives trying to convince themselves that their existence is not absurd."*
>
> —Albert Camus (1913-1960)

Chapter 2:
Ad Hominem

♦ ♦ ♦

Susan: "With recent terrorist attacks, I think it is fair to say we must increase military spending. There are many organizations that could be a threat to us and we need to defend ourselves from the threat of terrorism"

Henry: "Wow, Susan. I never knew you were a warmongering capitalist who supports the death and destruction created by these so-called wars. If you were smarter, you could think of a better way to deal with it."

Instead of attacking a person's argument and actually thinking about how to respond, a much easier approach is to just attack the other person. This is called the "ad hominem" fallacy and we <u>love</u> it. We target the person's character, motives, and other attributes. People who use this fallacy aren't credible; don't believe the statements they make.

Ad hominem means "to the man" in Latin. Equating someone's character with the validity of their arguments is a logical fallacy. However, don't confuse this with the concepts of "libel" and "slander". People slander each other when they make false statements to attack their opponents' reputations.

The next time you speak with someone and they bring up an incident from your past, recognize this as a perfect example of the ad hominem fallacy in action. Although your past actions may indicate your likely future actions, you are not defined by your past. Your personal history isn't the sole factor in deciding how you will behave in the present.

A good refutation of an argument undermines its accuracy, relevance, fairness, and completeness and persuades others to agree with you. When we are unable to do this, we may resort to attacking the other speaker. People who can't provide a good refutation of an argument divert attention away from this weakness by disparaging the other party. I'm sure we can all recall a time when pure frustration caused us to resort to this tactic.

Schoolyard "name calling" comes in many forms. Mentioning someone's sexual orientation or body shape doesn't add to your argument but it does give you a base psychological satisfaction. When we feel helpless, we often resort to ad hominem attacks to make ourselves feel better. If we can't argue with our boss directly about a new rule, we can say all manner of terrible things about her personality behind her back. We rarely gather around the water cooler and discuss how another person's point was more logical than our own.

Ad hominem attacks are very attractive to lazy thinkers who would rather ridicule or belittle others than critically analyze their own viewpoints. By not recognizing the merits of opposing viewpoints, we lose out on opportunities for greater clarity. Politicians love to use ad hominem attacks to play on people's emotions; voters are seduced into transmuting their disapproval for a candidate's personality trait (real or alleged) into total disagreement with that person's position.

This behavior may seem quite immature, but we adults don't realize how often we indulge in it. Campaign ads are perhaps the best examples of ad hominem attacks in action. In the 1991 U.S. Presidential race, a pro-Bush group attacked candidate Pat Buchanan by saying, "Buchanan tells us 'America First'. But, as our automotive industry suffers, he chooses to buy a foreign-made car—a Mercedes Benz. Pat Buchanan. It's 'America First' in his political speeches, but a foreign-made car in his driveway". As you can see, Pat Buchanan is clearly evil. Not only did he fail to purchase a gas-guzzling, notoriously-unreliable American car, he opted for a higher quality German automobile. Bush's statement effectively circumnavigates any form of logic and drives straight into his audience's <u>hearts</u>—not their minds. Emotional thinking doesn't reconcile well with reasoning; the result is a perfect example of the ad hominem attack.

Another example of an ad hominem attack comes to us from Alabama. The candidate, Dale Peterson, may not have won his position but his campaign ad would certainly have won an award for the "Most American Thing Ever". Peterson appears onscreen in typical American cowboy attire, including a large-brimmed hat, an oversized-belt buckle, a horse, and a visible firearm. He starts,

> "I'm Dale Peterson and I'm after a Republican nomination for the Alabama Agriculture Commission. I've been a farmer, businessman, cop, and Marine during Vietnam. So, listen up. Alabama Agriculture Commissioner is a

powerful job responsible for up to five billion dollars. I bet you didn't know that. You know why? Thugs and criminals. Here we are— illegals busting in by the thousands. Losing three family farms a day. Unemployment at an all-time high and what are my opponents doing about it? Stealing yard signs in the dark at night. Norman Gray brags on Facebook about receiving support from donors."

Peterson's campaign continues after three close ups of his rifle from various angles; he concludes with, "Let's show Alabama we mean business." Not only is this commercial highly entertaining, it is full of extreme ad hominem fallacies. Peterson made no mention of his opponent's actual stances on any relevant issues.

Attacking someone's motives instead of their evidence is tricky business, mostly because it's all based on supposition. We can't be certain of others' motives; we can only guess from biased information. Rather than taking part in a legitimate argument, it's easier to accuse a political opponent of "playing politics", taking bribes, or working for Big Pharma.

We accuse others of ad hominem attacks when we encounter decisions we don't like. Critics of judicial decisions often frame the judges' motives as biased. This is often found in legal contexts, where a person lacks a willingness to take responsibility and instead insinuates he or she is a victim of biased-judicial decisions.

Refuting an argument by claiming that the arguer stands to profit from a decision is a powerful way to reframe an opponent's position. This is a favorite method of conspiracy theorists. Despite an overwhelming amount of evidence to the contrary (and nearly every scientist on the planet's solid agreement on the effectiveness of vaccinations) some people don't trust the medical community. Armed with nothing more than a few YouTube videos and some non-scientific "facts", they have refuted the entire medical practice of vaccinations. They base this claim on the fact that physicians are paid for giving vaccinations and pharmaceutical firms profit from the sale of vaccines. Though this is true, these people provide a valuable service—namely, protecting us from diseases that killed most of early man. Arguments for anti-vaccination has ranged from Bill Gates using them for population control to ex-playmate Jenny McCarthy's accusations of vaccines causing autism.

The ad hominem fallacy is often used by proponents of pseudoscientific healing methods such as homeopathy, acupuncture, and distant healing. By focusing on the opposition to their healing practices, practitioners can reframe the modern-medical community as profiteers of medicine, vaccines, and expensive treatments. They call into question doctors' financial motives for prescribing medicines and divert attention from their own pseudoscience. They spin the idea that the medical community generates revenue by providing a valuable service into a strange "blame game".

These methods are all pretty standard. Now, it's time to teach you the trickiest of them all: Accusing the arguer of unjustly using the ad hominem attack! Calling someone "biased" before they can muster a defense is an excellent way to tilt the scales in your favor. The next time you're in an argument and you're pretty sure you're going to lose, remember this one trick: call the other person biased before they even have a chance to say anything.

Chapter 3:
Tu Quoque

♦ ♦ ♦

Sally: "You shouldn't eat that cheeseburger. Studies have shown that eating cheeseburgers late at night is terrible for your health"

Henry: "You eat cheeseburgers at night all the time. You ate one two-weeks ago."

In the Monty Python sketch, "I want to have an argument", a young John Cleese walks into an office and informs the receptionist he is looking to have an argument. The receptionist indicates that he needs to visit room 2B. Cleese walks into the first room and sits down. The other man in the room immediately engages in the pettiest argument possible. Whatever John says the man simply contradicts him by saying, "No, you didn't." After attempting to start a good argument, Cleese realizes he's stifled by the man's "You, too" and "No, you didn't" arguments, and decides to leave the room. Only upon leaving does he realize he was in the room labelled "contradiction" not "argument". This is the "tu quoque" argument (pronounced too-kwo-kwee for all non-native French speakers). Tu-quoque is an appeal to hypocrisy by taking the focus off of the person who should be defending against an argument and shifting the focus back onto the person making the initial claim. In the case of the Monty Python skit, the man in the contradiction room offers no critical thought whatsoever; instead, he launches into a series of cheap attacks.

People use the tu quoque fallacy to defend themselves from criticism by turning the critique back against the accuser. This distraction is also known as a "red herring"; whether the accuser is guilty of the same thing is irrelevant to the truth of the original charge. We engage in this tactic all the time; if you pay attention, you will definitely notice yourself using it. Tu quoque is basically an adult version of the childish, "I know you are, but what am I". This exceptionally-effective childhood defense system also works for adults. Shifting the blame is an excellent way to avoid responsibility without logic or proper reasoning; however, it also accomplishes another valuable task. In its true essence, tu quoque is a diversionary tactic that can put the other person on the defensive and make them feel compelled to defend against this accusation. Putting someone on the defensive stresses them and makes them more likely to make a weak statement that can easily be retorted.

Tu quoque is another common political tactic. Osama Bin Laden used when asked if he was still funding terrorist training camps and sponsoring international terrorism. He said, "Wherever we look, we find the U.S. as the leader of terrorism and crime in the world. The U.S. does not consider it a terrorist act to throw atomic bombs at nations thousands of miles away, when it would not be possible for those bombs to hit military troops only. These bombs were rather thrown at entire nations— including women, children and elderly people—and up to this day the traces of those bombs remain in Japan".[xvi] Mr.

Bin Laden never actually addressed the question of whether he sponsored terrorism; instead, he turned the question back on his accuser. Bin Ladin's irrelevancy is designed to distract his audience from the question at hand—his sponsorship of terrorism. The facts he mentioned are true; however, they had no bearing on the question of whether or not he promoted terrorism. This idea is often incorporated in tu quoque, "if you can do it, so can I". This argument is not only immoral—it's terrible illogic. Using others' previous actions as justifications for what you want to do is an attempt to escape responsibility. This technique is often used by children: when restricted from doing something, they mention that their parents have done the same thing. Fortunately, children aren't aware of logical fallacies and such arguments can quickly be ended with an illogical, "Because I said so".

The Soviet Union used tu quoque as a fundamental political tactic. During the cold war, the Western media described this Russian political tactic as "whataboutism". The Soviet Union's media matched Soviet crimes and blunders with references to (real or imaged) Western ones. In 1986, the Soviet Union belatedly announced the Chernobyl incident (after Western countries had already detected an unusually high amount of radioactivity). Upon hearing Western news sources report on the disaster, the Soviet Union made an official statement that included the following, "There have been many mishaps in the United States, ranging from Three Mile Island outside Harrisburg, PA to the Ginna plant near Rochester. An American antinuclear group registered 2,300 accidents, breakdowns, and other faults in 1979."[xvii]

Instead of taking responsibility, the Russians simply mentioned a plethora of U.S. mistakes and carried on like nothing had happened. Now, I don't suggest you use this method in your own life. Just because the Russians can do it doesn't mean you can, right? Listing and remembering all of your friends' mistakes as ammunition for future arguments will only make you look crazy.

However, the Russians didn't stop there. They developed a common anecdotal counter-argument phrase as a responses to allegations of human rights abuse. Although the Soviet Union had clearly violated many people's human rights, they attempted to distract the public by mentioning the treatment of African Americans. The Russian saying, "А у вас негров вешают" meaning "And you are hanging blacks"[xviii] attempted to focus on America's human rights record and evade Western pressure to fess up to their own human rights violations.

Although tu quoque is a fancy-sounding name, it is very common. This fallacy has been the centerpiece of morality tales throughout the ages. The sayings, "Two wrongs don't make a right" and "The pot calling the kettle black" are both good examples of this. The idea of "The pot calling the kettle black" originated in an early issue of "St. Nicholas Magazine". The accuser (the pot) shares some qualities with the target of its accusations. In this tale, the arrogant pot mocks the smaller kettle for having a little soot on it, even though the pot is covered in it.

When you read about such tactics, it's not difficult to see them as childish. However, tu quoque is a part of our cultural landscape, from the schoolyard to the highest-echelon of politics. Be careful, almost any argument can devolve into a "You, too" type of name-calling match.

Chapter 4:
The Straw Man

♦ ♦ ♦

Susan: "We should set up more bike lanes in San Francisco because it's a healthy alternative to driving. It's a great form of transportation."

Henry: "That isn't a good idea. Bicyclists run red lights, endanger pedestrians, and block traffic. I don't think we should."

This one is subtle, and difficult to notice. People can restate your point in a slightly-reframed manner that allows them to dismantle your argument. Why take on a real man with flesh and bones when we can destroy a wimpy "straw" opponent. Like a punching — weakly constructed arguments can be dismantled and the other person can appear wrong.

The "straw man" argument is derived from a military term used to baffle the enemy with fake soldiers. As the name describes, it's a deliberate misrepresentation. This can be achieved in a number of ways: One of the most widely used methods involves "framing". Framing is a process in which a particular argument or point is presented in a slightly-skewed context; this can lead to an eventual agreement or disagreement on a point. Ideas don't exist alone; they live in a symbiotic web of meaning that is represented by images, memories, ideas, and people. By quoting people out-of-context, we can shift the context in a direction that suits our purposes. Excluding key points and details is also an effective way of attenuating or exaggerating the feeling of an argument.

When we employ straw man arguments, we often hold onto a weak defense and represent it as the entire defensive argument. By focusing on one particularly stupid or inconsequential point, we attempt to prove we are right—and the other person guilty of some error in logic. I'm sure we can all think of a personal encounter in which we have over-emphasized a point just to enhance our position. We emphasize something that was previously unimportant to gain ammunition for an attack. Focusing on an unimportant point and inflating its relevance is a common manifestation of the straw man argument. The need to be right dictates that we need something to hold on to.

Another straw man tactic is to highlight and focus on the most extreme points made by the opposition. For example, if I were to say it's important to teach sex education to teenagers in public schools, this argument could be rebutted by saying that such an "education" only serves to give children the license to have sex without responsibility. By focusing on only one facet of a multi-faceted situation, we attempt to simplify the cause-and-effect relationship. When causality is simplified like this—and presented in an incomplete and easy-to-refute form—a difficult argument becomes much easier.

The straw man argument is often used in the political arena. In recent years, conservative pundits have regularly called President Obama a "Socialist" whenever he proposes a government action. Despite the fact that this isn't true, Obama's proposals on health care, bailouts, and other government interventions make him a great target for this kind of attack. However, in politics, the easiest way to construct a straw man argument is with a generous application of stereotypes. The President's critics have said, "Obama wants to seize the money of hardworking Americans and redistribute it to single mothers and jobless crackheads ... until we resemble the Soviet Union."[xix] Considering such ludicrous statements such as the one above distracts us from the overall argument and prevents the discussion of real issues.

Debates about religion and evolution are also rife with straw-man attacks. Conflating religions together into one entity or exaggerating various aspects of a religious practice make them easier to refute. Both sides of this debate often use straw-man arguments. When we talk about large groups of people, it is easy to lump them into one archetype and present an argument against them. By lumping various religions together, we can easily dismiss a generic "straw man" version of religion. The same can be done to atheists.

The problem with lumping groups of people together is that becomes impossible to make an accurate assessment; instead, we must use a hypothetical one. This involves one of the more common cognitive biases – the "availability bias". This bias makes us rely on immediate examples that come to our minds when evaluating specific topics, concepts, methods, or decisions. We often fail to use proper reasoning and instead form a straw man argument based on recently available information.

In another strange twist of straw man logic, a debating technique known as the "Gish Gallop" can be applied with annoying efficiency. The idea is simple—to drown a person in an endless series of "small, but poor" arguments—so many that the opponent cannot possibly answer or address them. These arguments are typically a large variety of straw-man allegations. They don't have to be good—they just need to be many.

As a child, I quickly discovered the Gish Gallop technique. I just wish someone had told me its name. This was one of my favorite childhood tactics to use against my mother; it was particularly effective while she driving. After bombarding her with an endless onslaught of requests for permission, I would follow up with hypothetical questions. The hypothetical questions was where she would give in. I now realize that my questions were all slight variations of straw man arguments. I would ask: If you did this, then, how about X? Or if this didn't happen, then would you X? Eventually the brain power and patience required to answer all my questions was just too much, instead she just acquiesced to my demands.

This kind of argument has become extremely popular over the last 10 years. The "listicle", which usually starts with a heading like "50 Reasons Why" or "100 Ways to" basically repeats the same points with slight variations. The logic behind it is simple; if you wanted to refute the entire premise of the article, you would have to refute fifty little points. This is why bullet points are so effective: the sheer amount of points you would have to address becomes overwhelming. Most people just give up and don't disagree.

In debate, this technique is called "spreading". The idea is simple – throw as much bullshit as you can at the opponent in your allotted time. The person who can deflect the most verbose crap and escape unscathed wins. Now, you would think that shooting out straw man arguments left and right would make you appear incompetent. However, research on audiences that observe this style of debate show the opposite to be true. Research shows that people who aren't conscious of this technique actually mistake it for a person's wide-range of knowledge on the subject.[11]

Sometimes a proposed straw man argument is so stupid that even beginning to refute it brings you down to a losing level. Let me introduce the "Peanut Butter Argument". Creationist Chuck Missler attempted to use this evidence to discredit the Theory of Evolution. Missler argued, "As life does not evolve spontaneously in sealed jars of peanut butter, it is absurd to assume it evolved spontaneously on the primordial Earth."[xx] If this example doesn't actually hurt your head, please go back and reread it. I'm not sure which part is more shocking, that someone actually wrote this with serious intent—or that other people actually believe it. In a beautiful video, Missler explains that matter and energy combine to form life, that peanut butter also contain matter, and that is can be exposed to energy in the form of light. He argues that, despite the requirements of matter and energy being met, we never see life forming inside a peanut butter jar. Missler mentions this with astonishment, considering the millions of people who regularly consume peanut butter. Since no life forms have sprung forth within the jar, he says, evolution is a fairy-tale and intelligent design must be true. I won't even begin to attempt to understand this; however, it is an extreme example of how the need to be right can compel individuals to create straw man stories which are so absurd they can actually make your brain hurt.

In a your battle against "men of straw" there is one main problem; they don't fight back. Straw men don't wear armor, don't bleed, and generally aren't like anything you've encountered before. Therefore, arguing against a straw man isn't like debating with a real person; it's an idealized fiction in another person's mind. The straw man has an amorphous shape which can change direction at any moment. The creators of straw man arguments do little more than extend their opponent's arguments beyond the original point until their premises seems absurd.

There is a "turning point" that makes straw man arguments particularly effective. In essence, you're fighting a battle in which the odds are very much against you. The second you engage with a straw man argument (by refuting it or arguing against it) you have given it validity as an argument and entered into an impossible-to-win situation. You cannot defend against an argument that isn't based on anything—and can be quickly changed at will. The next time you encounter a situation in which your story is being reframed, exercise caution. Make sure your argument is being described accurately and isn't being replaced with a cheap grass reconstruction.

Chapter 5:
Burden of Proof

♦ ♦ ♦

Sally: "Look at the pyramids. There's no way ancient people built those—they were surely made by aliens."

Henry: "What's your proof?"

Sally: "Look how big they are. No one has ever been able to prove they weren't made by aliens."

"Russel's Teapot" is an analogy constructed by British philosopher Bertrand Russell. This analogy comes in the form of a thought experiment that illustrates "burden of proof" and how easily it can be used to falsify information. Russell states,

> "If I were to suggest that between the Earth and Mars there is a China teapot revolving about the sun in an elliptical orbit, nobody would be able to disprove my assertion provided I were careful to add that the teapot is too small to be revealed even by our most powerful telescopes. But if I were to go on to say that, since my assertion cannot be disproved, it is an

intolerable presumption on the part of human reason to doubt it, I should rightly be thought to be talking nonsense. If, however, the existence of such a teapot were affirmed in ancient books, taught as the sacred truth every Sunday, and instilled into the minds of children at school, hesitation to believe in its existence would become a mark of eccentricity and entitle the doubter to the attentions of the psychiatrist in an enlightened age or of the Inquisitor in an earlier time." [xxi]

Now, there may be an alien teapot floating innocently in space—but this is quite unlikely. Russell proposed this ridiculous situation to exemplify the fallacy known as "burden of proof". This fallacy occurs when the burden of proof lies not with the person making the claim, but with those refuting it. In reality, both people should provide evidence of their opinions.

Most assumptions we make in our lives aren't based on any good, solid evidence. Instead, we rely mostly on hearsay and second-hand information. Making a claim and supporting it with solid evidence is your responsibility. When we place the burden of proof on the opposite side, we frame their inability to provide evidence as a *lack of evidence*. There is an uneven requirement to show proof: the side making the claim is exempt from providing any evidence since they are making a claim that is assumed to be true.

If I were to make an outrageous claim like, "The moon is made of cheese—I want to eat some of it," you would hopefully inform me that the moon was certainly not made of cheese. It would be my responsibility to validate this claim, perhaps letting you sample a small-but-delicious portion of mooncheese. However, with the proof of burden fallacy, you are left with the responsibility of disproving my claim.

Determining where the burden of proof lies can be difficult and often requires legal intervention. The most common manifestation of this is the idea that you are assumed innocent until proven guilty. This axiom of Western law places the burden of proof on the prosecution. Our legal system is based on this idea; most distortions of the law occur when we violate this principle. Accusations require evidence, whereas the person who does not carry the burden of proof carries the benefit of assumption. Thankfully, our legal system has rigorous checks and balances to evaluate and verify the quality of evidence used to make decisions. Burden of proof must not only be abundant—it must also be verifiable. I can't present a terrible reason for my opposition to your position and expect to be believed; I must prove beyond a reasonable doubt that you are indeed incorrect.

However, history has not always shown this level of fairness towards required proof. The "burden" of providing solid evidence hasn't always been of paramount importance. Take the Salem Witch Trials or the Inquisition for example: medieval systems listed specific parameters for identifying, trying, and even executing suspected evil magic practitioners. Unfortunately for the suspects, these tests weren't very exactly fair. The "swimming test" involved stripping suspected witches, binding them to heavy objects, and throwing them into a lake. If they defied the laws of physics and somehow didn't sink, they were not witches. Conveniently, if they drowned, they were witches. If this test didn't work, there was always the "witch cake", which was a supernatural dessert used to identify black magic. It was a simple mixture of the victim's urine, rye-meal, and ashes. After being baked to perfection, it was fed to a dog. The dog was known as a "familiar" or a beast who helped witches. After enjoying the urine/rye/ash dog biscuit, the canine co-conspirator was observed for any strange noises or "confessions". It was believed that the beast would fall under the witch's spell and reveal the name of the guilty sorcerer. Modern burden of proof doesn't require dogs to consume urine cakes or being asked to defy the laws of object buoyancy. However, using an intentionally absurd analogy like Russell's Teapot, we can draw attention to the burden of proof works.

The next time someone makes a false claim and you feel the need to refute it, know that you may be required to produce contrary evidence. Smartphones and 24/7 Internet access make it simple; just whip out Google and search "topic+science based" to find a plethora of information that exonerates your claim and disproves your opponents'. To battle the burden of proof fallacy we must also ask the opposition to present information that supports their opinion and not ride on the coat-tails of "assumption".

In 1748, philosopher David Hume wrote, "A wise man proportions his beliefs to the evidence". This sentence has become an axiom of scientific thought. If someone makes claims that seem beyond the realm of possibility, it is up to them to provide evidence of equally amazing quality. The renowned Carl Sagan popularized the phrase, "Extraordinary claims require extraordinary evidence." Sagan also demonstrated the power of the burden of proof and how it contributes to the falsifiability of claims. Carl proposed an analogy of an invisible-undetectable dragon living in someone's garage. You couldn't physical tell it was there, but it was. Sagan's analogy demonstrates another fallacy, known as "moving the goal post". This occurs when your previously agreed upon standards for deciding an argument are arbitrarily changed.

When I make a ridiculous claim, you open the doorway to two logical aberrations. The first is by using a claim so ridiculous and impossible your opponents are unable to prove it using "real" evidence. Second, this inability to disprove your argument makes the initial absurd evidence seem somehow more valid! If the person refuting your logic issues equally ridiculous examples, you may call them out on the inaccuracy of their statements and spare yourself the same scrutiny.

A person's inability to invalidate my hypothesis is not the same as proving it's true. If a claim cannot be tested and its assertions are immune to disproof, it is worthless. So, what can we learn from claims far removed from reality? They represent a powerful human need to validate our worldview and maintain our position as "correct". Our own belief systems aren't subject to the examination and scrutiny we reserve for opposing belief systems. By pointing the finger of burden at another, we escape self-reflection and pass off the burden of proof to others.

The burden of proof fallacy often arises in religious arguments. Any arguments involving opposing belief systems give this fallacy considerable strength. People who hold belief systems and make claims about strange powers and otherworldly sources of influence that cannot be verified or evaluated by earthly methods are attempting to escape the burden of proof. People often believe that belief systems are "different" and don't require the same evidence. However, such proposals are also similar to the claim made by Russell—a lack of evidence beyond the conviction of its existence.

Arguments for unprovable belief systems are actually

weaker than the case of the floating interstellar teapot. The teapot, at least (if it actually existed) would not purposely violate any known physical laws. Belief systems that encourage ideas that exist beyond the realm of possible physical phenomenon require even more extraordinary proof than just a misplaced teapot. Unfortunately, we rarely examine or compare events with this level of skepticism.

This lack of skepticism is often the result of our social beliefs. No one would believe such absurd nonsense as a moon made of cheese or a flying teapot when it is proposed in such an unfamiliar way. However, when we encounter equally absurd belief systems in socially or historically-familiar contexts, they seem to have a measure of proof and be established or valid. In other words, a lot of people believing some total bullshit creates a form of social proof.

Chapter 6:
Slippery Slope

♦ ♦ ♦

Janet: "We don't let our son go out—if we do, he might meet some bad friends. If he meets some bad friends, it'll only be a matter of time before he starts using drugs. Once his drug addiction is fully formed, he'll start robbing people for additional drug-money. Eventually, he'll die. Therefore, we don't let our son leave the house."

In the 2016 election battle, we had the pleasure once again of meeting Virginia-born Rick Santorum, a lawyer who once defended the World Wrestling Federation. He had been on both sides of the debate regarding gay rights; however, a 2003 interview made his views on gay marriage quite clear. The debate involved the Lawrence vs Texas case[xxii], which invalidated laws the forbid private, consensual sexual activities. In a follow-up interview, Santorum said,

> "Every society in the history of man has upheld the institution of marriage as a bond between a man and a woman. Why? Because society is based on one thing. And that's what? Children. Monogamous relationships. In every society, the

definition of marriage has not ever to my knowledge included homosexuality. That's not to pick on homosexuality. It's not, you know, man on child, man on dog, or whatever the case may be. And when you destroy that you have a dramatic impact on the quality."[xxiii]

In case you missed it, Santorum associated the acceptance of gay rights with bestiality. While this extreme example immediately comes across as ridiculous, it demonstrates a common fallacy – the "slippery slope".

Like a giant snowball tumbling down a hill, a slippery slope argument starts small, picks up a series of unjustified assumptions along the way, and forms into a lumbering ball of bullshit. In this logical fallacy, a person claims one event will be followed by another—without any rational argument or demonstrable mechanism for arriving at this conclusion.

The idea of a small step that sets in motion a series of events that culminate in a significant outcome has some validity. When we achieve a measure of success in our lives, this often seems to manifest as a domino-effect of outcomes and conditions. In retrospect, we often see our past events and decisions as the inevitable outcomes of a series of "random events" and "chance encounters". As we try to understand our worlds, we look to the past and project our need for meaning onto past events by giving them a "preordained" quality. Things "happen for a reason" because we <u>want</u> them to have happened for a reason. This way, when we look back in time, the events and conditions that led us to our current position in life make sense. We also apply this logic to the future; however, our forecasting models are often incorrect. The slippery slope is a perfect example of a "forecasting model" gone wrong.

The slippery slope is exemplified by George Costanza's mother in the hit T.V. show, "Seinfeld". She is neurotically overprotective and attacks George with an unending barrage of slippery slope arguments. While something bad may happen; its possibility of occurring is based entirely on the strength of its premises.

A good argument's strength is based on its "warrant". A warrant is one's ability to demonstrate a process that leads to a significant outcome. If I argued that drinking an entire bottle of vodka would get you drunk, my warrant would be that the *process* (drinking all of it) will lead to an *outcome* (you get very drunk). A warrant is only logically sound if it is highly demonstrable. When we depart from this level of solid evidence, we can accept slippery slope arguments and "fear mongering". In this condition, we perceive the small probability of a negative outcome as much larger than it really is.

Another good example of the slippery slope fallacy is in the rhetoric of some opponents to drug and alcohol use. The idea that getting drunk or high, just once, is enough to create a powerful addiction and ruin one's life is a primary assumption of many anti-drug ads. A classic example of this is the 1987 "This is your brain on drugs" ad campaign (that was funded by a huge amount of American tax dollars). In an attempt to illustrate the shocking reality of drug abuse, a man appears on camera in an upscale kitchen. He walks to the stove, picks up a frying pan and says, "This is your brain". He then motions to the frying pan and says, "This is drugs". The man breaks open an egg and drops it into the hot frying pan, where it sizzles and cooks. He concludes by holding up the delicious fried egg and saying, "This is your brain on drugs. Any questions?" Although it is difficult to refute such precise logic, one can clearly see the slippery slope in action. The insinuation that your brain is in fact a delicious egg waiting to be eaten is not only horrifying, it also demonstrates a powerful truth: when our emotions are activated, we are susceptible to massive gaps in logic.

Though we often aren't aware of it, we often apply the slippery slope fallacy to our daily decisions. We make the mistake of equating correlation with causation; in other words, just because a cause contributed to an effect, it's not necessarily the sole, originating cause of that effect. The world is complicated; we can't determine most causation factors. To increase our decision-making abilities, we can regularly ask ourselves this question: "Am I sure about this? Or am I just making an assumption?"

Upon repeated examination, you will find that the majority of decisions in life are not made with logical evaluation and honest reflection. Instead, we make choices based on "handed-down" or socially-enforced assumptions. This behavior leaves us particularly vulnerable to slippery slope arguments and biases; when we don't think through our decisions well enough, we are easily persuaded by others' fear-mongering tactics. If we hand over our responsibility for determining the truth to the people around us, open ourselves up to a world of negative influences.

Another aspect (that makes the slippery slope even more slippery) is the ability of hypothetical arguments to go either way. In most slippery slope cases, no evidence is presented. This opens up an ability to argue either way. If I were to use Santorum's tactics when he implies the eventual outcome of accepting gay marriage is man-on-dog sex, I could argue that banning gay marriage would be eventually be followed by a ban on marriage in general. Both of arguments are equally impossible; however, they demonstrate how the slippery slope can be used on either side of an argument.

It is tempting to use slippery slope tactics. When we aren't restricted by the need for evidence or logical boundaries, our innate desire to "be right" comes out in full force. Be on the lookout— the slippery slope argument is available for everyone to use (and often to comic effect) However, people with expert persuasion skills can trick us into accepting this fallacy.

Chapter 7:
Anecdotal Evidence

♦ ♦ ♦

Let's cover some homemade remedies for multi-causal medical symptoms. These may seem silly to us today, but they were the "go-to" methods of doctors in the 1700s.[xxiv]

1. Suffering from the Falling Disease?

Falling disease causes people to convulse all over, become utterly senseless, grind their teeth, and produce all manner of strange secretions from their mouths. Luckily, there is a simple cure: A diet consisting only of milk for three months rarely fails; and, in case of a serious fit, just put some ginger into the patient's nose.

2. Cure the Quinsy.

If you're unfamiliar with 1700s medical terminology, let me describe "Quinsy". The symptoms of this condition include fever followed by difficulty breathing and swallowing. However, there is a sure-fire cure for this malady: simply apply a large piece of white bread (dipped in brandy) to the patient's forehead until it dries. No more Quinsy.

3.   Got Gout?

Gout in the foot or hand can be especially frustrating. This condition can be cured by applying a raw, lean beef steak to the affected area. Leave it on the area for twelve hours—or until the gout is cured.

Humans love stories; we can't get enough of them. We love them to the point of confusing them with reality and believing they actually represent reliable evidence. These are anecdotes; this chapter describes the "anecdotal fallacy". When we use anecdotes to support or refute a claim, we are guilty of this bias. Anecdotes often come in the form of "hearsay evidence", personal stories, or second-hand information.

Relying on anecdotes to make a point makes sense for two reasons. First, when we talk with people, we often share stories; these stories often contain faulty reasoning (in their causal factors). We are unable to access the validity of the claims people make in stories and generally assume these personal anecdotes are true. When talking with others, we rarely exchange pie charts, statistically-significant values, and discuss the potential biases in our experimental design. Instead, we just believe people and their stories. Second, personal stories affect us on an emotional level. Hearing an anecdote of an event that made a person incredibly happy or hurt will trigger our powerful emotional needs to be respected, avoid pain, and maintain safety. These anecdotes may belong to someone else, but we interpret them through the framework of our own personal history; these stories become infused with our own subjective meanings.

Anecdotal evidence is often the starting point for real scientific research. Hearing an anecdote about an unexplained phenomenon could inspire a scientist to study it. The researcher may quickly refute the anecdote as pseudoscience or rework it to more accurately explain the event. "Pseudoscientists" love anecdotes. To these people, an anecdote has the same validity as a double-blind, peer-reviewed, scientific experiment. Since this happened to someone they know, it must be possible and therefore, repeatable. Anecdotes are nice illustrative stories that do <u>not</u> constitute evidence.

A story isn't an objective narration of an event; it has gone through a person's subjective filter (or many people's filters) and is subject to bias. If I told you my uncle Johnny is 65 years old, works out twice a day, has a six-pack, can bench 350, and eats nothing but bacon grease, raw vegetables, and fish—would that seem like believable evidence? When you read this story in a book about logical reasoning, it seems silly. However, we often encounter equally ridiculous arguments in real life. You can see anecdotal evidence everywhere: in journalism, politics, online information, and personal stories. We are likely to perceive these "cherry-picked" examples as more reliable than statistical evidence.

Who can blame us for not wanting to read statistics? They're <u>boring</u>. Here's a great business idea for you—make statistics fun and exciting. This would eliminate the possibility of widespread manipulation—as in the classic Ronald Reagan story. In a memorable 1976 speech, Ronald Reagan describing a character he called a "welfare queen". This women made her living by scamming her way into veteran's benefits and social security payments from four fake deceased husbands.[xxv] In one instance, she scammed the government for over $8,000. This "welfare queen" was <u>not</u> your average welfare recipient; she was also suspected of murder and kidnapping. However, this example spurred a wave of welfare-recipient stereotypes that were founded on nothing but crazy anecdotal evidence like the "welfare queen".

Research has shown that people are more likely to remember notable examples than typical examples.[xxvi] A notable event creates an emotional reaction that makes an experience more salient than usual. When someone tells a story, we feel empathy and mirror their emotions. We don't look at the relevant statistics and exclaim, "Oh my God! It's statistically significant" or "My results fall three standard deviations from the mean!" Numbers aren't interesting to the average person—but stories are exciting. These personal anecdotes are called "testimonials" in the business world—and they work. Although anecdotal evidence is not accepted as proper proof in science or law, strong narratives hold convincing power that resonates with people on a personal level.

A skilled story teller can bring you into their world: as you become involved in each of the twists and turns of a story, you imagine yourself in it. You begin to ask yourself, "How do the characters feel?", "What would I do in this situation?", and "What might happen?" We fill in these blanks as we listen to stories, piecing the various parts together in our minds. A story "sticks with us" because it creates a powerful bond that facts and numbers simply can't provide.

One of the best demonstrations of this is the "vaccine hysteria". Even in this day and age (and despite the fact that the medical community is united on the importance of vaccines), a small subset of people believe vaccines are dangerous. This vaccine analogy demonstrates the "two sides" of the anecdotal fallacy: On one side is strong, reproducible, and highly-rigorous scientific evidence; on the other is a group of people armed with an array of personal narratives about vaccine-related sicknesses and deaths. For some people, anecdotal stories are more compelling than science.

Anecdotes are strengthened when their results are so unlikely, they "couldn't have been a coincidence". For example, your cousin Bernie was terribly ill for over 3 weeks. However, one day, he decided to eat three bowls of sour cream. Surprisingly, he was fully recovered the next day—the sour cream must have cured him! If this anecdote is passed on long enough, and by enough people, it can gain validity and become not only an anecdote, but an <u>anecdote from the past</u>. People often judge stories' veracity by their longevity.

This fallacy is often employed by supporters of alternative medicine. Millions of sick and dying people have tried alternative medicines. Some of these people get well; however, this doesn't mean that these alternative remedies caused them to heal. Most of the time, these "healings" are the results of coincidence. If enough people play the lottery, someone will win; however, the methods they used to pick their winning numbers aren't magic—it's simply the "luck of the draw".

Anecdotes of this nature don't prove anything. A statement like, "My uncle smoked until he was 80 and he was still healthy" may be true; however, this person is definitely an exception to the rule. Claims in which a factor affects (and uniquely determines) the probability of an outcome are useless and shouldn't be regarded as solid evidence. A statistical correlation between two events doesn't prove that one caused the other, rather that there may be a causal link. For example, research has shown that people's sugar consumption increases with their television viewing time.[xxvii] This shows a causal link; however, it doesn't prove that watching television increases your sugar intake.

The next time someone tells you a story, don't disbelieve them; however, please exercise skepticism. We use stories to bring others over to our side. The problem lies in the ways we process information. When we encounter a new piece of information, we rarely stop and rationally analyze it; instead, we process this new information with heuristics. These cognitive "rules of thumb" provide mental shortcuts that allow us to make faster decisions. One of these mental shortcuts, the "availability heuristic", makes anecdotal evidence particularly easy to remember: the easier it is to remember or imagine an event, the more likely we perceived it to occur. We remember certain things in our experience better than others; because we remember those events, we think they're more likely to happen. For example, if you've heard about a recent accident, you'll be much more likely to drive safely and use your seatbelt than if you hadn't been primed by such examples. Your brain interprets "ease of recall" as an additional source of information. Easy-to-remember events are perceived as more salient—and more believable.

When an event is surprising, dangerous, or exciting, our resulting emotional reaction causes this memory to be embedded in a much deeper level of mind than usual. Memories are embedded in our brains via a network of previous representations, images, experiences, and concepts. The more connections we make, the deeper a memory is "embedded". Emotional events activate more areas of the brain and facilitate deeper embedding. The emotional power of an event can be used as a metric for evaluating and event's validity. These factors work together to bias our perception of an event's probability. In this vast area of research, the results are fairly concrete: humans are absolutely terrible at guessing probabilities. We rely on exceptions and anecdotal evidence when imagining what may or may not happen.

Our anecdotes are unreliable for many reasons:

- We contaminate our stories with our beliefs and experiences.
- We change our facts based on feedback from others.
- We pay selective attention to detail.
- We distort stories the more we tell and re-tell them.
- We exaggerate events and confuse time sequences.
- We muddle up the details and often "fill in the details" after an experience.
- We misinterpret our experiences and have "selective memories".
- We condition our experiences with our biases, memories, and beliefs.

Most listeners aren't expecting to be deceived, they may not even be aware of others' deception. Some people make up stories; some stories are delusions. Sometimes, we deem events "psychic" simply because they feel improbable—when they might not be that improbable at all. In short, anecdotes are inherently problematic and are usually impossible to test for accuracy. [xxviii]

Chapter 8:
The Black-and-White Fallacy

♦ ♦ ♦

"Honesty may be the best policy, but it's important to remember that apparently, by elimination, dishonesty is the second-best policy."

—George Carlin

If you're wrong, I am right?

Does that logic make sense? Not necessarily.

While your opinion or position may be invalid, it mean mine is correct. This is the "black-and-white" fallacy. This fallacy is so widespread that it has about fifteen different names, including the "false dilemma". Some of the more common names are: false dichotomy, false binary, black-and-white thinking, bifurcation, denying a conjunct, the either–or fallacy, fallacy of exhaustive hypotheses, the fallacy of false choice, the fallacy of the false alternative, or the fallacy of the excluded middle. When you are forced to choose between two choices, despite the fact that other options exist, you enter into a "dilemma of choice". Which one should you pick? Instead of analyzing all of the available choices, we often narrowly focus only on two options. When our alternatives are limited, we are forced into decisions that we might not otherwise make. Differences between only two options become polarizing forces. In politics, the black-and-white fallacy leads us to falsely assume that if we support A, we must disagree with B—and that we can't exist in the middle.

This fallacy is often forced on people who must "choose a sides". It's embodied in the phrase, "If you aren't with us, you're against us". This "Balkanizing" form of thinking forces people to pick sides and make personal affirmations of the side they identify with. Let's look at another example to gain some clarity: If I were to tell a fellow employee, "I used to think you were a good person, but you didn't come to the charity event yesterday", I'm forcing this person into a false dilemma. If they accept what I said and validates it with a response, they've been tricked into explaining their actions. Skilled persuaders can easily use this fallacy to slip past your logical guard and force you into an uncomfortable scenario.

However, the psychology of he false dilemma extends deeper. When you're forced into this fallacy, you must pick a side. Identifying with a side means you've adopted a stance and must defend it. By selecting one side over another, you're making an affirmation. According to self-perception theory, our actions and behaviors must align with our value systems; otherwise, we would experience cognitive dissonance. By affirming that we support a certain position, we integrate it within our value systems; it becomes a value that we resonate and identify with.

The black-and-white fallacy can be a result of the accidental omission of other choices—or the result of a deliberate deception. This fallacy plays on the logical process itself; therefore, it is one of the trickiest to detect.

The false dilemma is an aberration of the "formal fallacy" or "logical fallacy". It violates a rule of propositional calculus. Don't be frightened by the term "calculus". It's actually quite simple: a fallacy of this nature can be determined as invalid simply by examining the form and structure of the argument. To truly understand this concept, you must know what a "syllogism" is. A syllogism is a logical argument that arrives at a conclusion determined by two "premises". These premises are asserted to be true. A good syllogism preserves the truth of its premises. If the premises are true, the conclusion can be considered true. However, if any of the premises are faulty, the conclusion that is reached is inaccurate. Think of this example: Lazy people don't pass exams. However, some students in your class often pass the exam. Therefore, some of the students in your class aren't lazy.

Syllogisms are the most basic tools of "logic". They form what is known as "Classical" or "Aristotelian" logic. (The term "logic" was actually created by Aristotle.) The black-and-white fallacy piggybacks on this logical process with two important exceptions: First, the premises are often inaccurate or based on biased information – making the conclusion invalid. Second, there may be more than two options—making any decision tenuous.

Unless you have a sharp mind, a skilled speaker can deceive you with this fallacy. Let's examine their trick:

Example 1:

1. Sia is a man.
2. All men are mortal.

3.   Therefore, Sia is a mortal.

This makes sense. The proposition is correct and it also reflects evidence we can see in reality. Both of these premises (#1 and #2) are correct and our natural inference (#3) is valid and follows a logical syllogistic structure. These statements are solid and the inferences we make from them are also valid.

So, what happens if we use the same structure to produce an inference that is both illogical and invalid:

Example 2:

1. Sia is a man.
2. All men are green.
3. Therefore, Sia is green.

In this example, the second statement is false; however, the form and structure of this argument is correct. The assumption we make in #3 demonstrates a formal logical fallacy. Formal fallacies are "invalid arguments"— arguments in which the conclusion does not necessarily follow the statements preceding it. In this case, I am not green. When you make conclusions based on unexamined and unsubstantiated premises, they will be wrong.

You can find many examples of this in your life—and in society. The popular false dilemma of "Love America or Leave It", is a good example of the black-and-white fallacy. In this case, a "true patriot" embraces everything American and those find any fault with the country are clearly un-American. This fallacy was exemplified by George W. Bush in his "War on Terror" speech. He said, "Either you are with us, or you are with the terrorists". Not only did this ridiculous statement insinuate that anyone who didn't support his widespread military intervention was a traitor; it also forced people into a logical fallacy. When we face a complicated issue like killing people in other countries—creating a fallacy that forces people into polarized factions destroys the rational decision-making process. When premises are biased or incorrect, the resulting decision is also warped. Bush's "War on Terror" was a misnomer. He had no identifiable enemy ("terror" is not a person, it's an emotion); it's also virtually impossible to eradicate international terrorism with military force.

When we continuously define a problem with false dilemmas, we risk a great danger; permanently defining that situation as only two-sided. The debate over Israel is a good example of this. Arguments by groups critical of the state of Israeli and Israeli policies are considered to be both Anti-Zionist and Anti-Semitic. While a person may disagree with Israeli policies, they may not be anti-Semitic in any way; however, when filtered through this black-and-white fallacy, this person could be are associated with "the other side".

Throughout religious history, people have used false dilemmas to make decisions—albeit irrational ones. French philosopher, mathematician, and physicist Blase Bascal explained the religious incentive for false dilemmas with an idea he coined "Pascal's Wager". Pascal said humans bet their lives on the idea that God either exists, or does not. Based on the assumption that the stakes are infinite, a rational person would live as through God existed—to avoid eternal torment and pain. If God didn't exist, this person would suffer only a finite loss (time, energy, tithing, etc.). However, they stand to receive infinite gains (and avoid infinite pain and loss) if God <u>does</u> exist. "Pascal's Wager" made sense to rational minded people in the 1600s; many of his contemporaries agreed with him. However, what Pascal didn't factor in was that his God was assumed to have ultimate authority over the myriad of other possible deities; Pascal dismissed such possibilities in favor of a simple two-sided decision.

The next time you're presented with an argument and only given two sides to choose from—consider the black-and-white fallacy. Some decisions can't be broken down into only two "sides"; however, in our need to persuade others to agree with and join our positions, we often use this faulty logic.

The false dilemma might be a fallacy but it also describes something very human—our need to simplify our worlds into easily understandable parts. Separating decisions into only <u>two</u> parts makes them much easier. Decisions are often messy and require us to examine a host of options; choosing between "this and that" provides a sense of neatness that helps us make sense of life. When you make important decisions, know that being forced into a dilemma can influence you to make an irrational choice. As Darth Vader told Obi-Wan Kenobi in Star Wars: Episode III, "If you aren't with me, then you're my enemy". To this, the courageous Obi-Wan retorted, "Only a Sith Lord deals in absolutes."

Chapter 9:

The Bandwagon Fallacy

♦ ♦ ♦

"Eat shit. Twenty trillion flies can't be wrong."

—Bill Maher

- Enjoy a tasty, radioactive beverage!
- How about some good old-fashioned uranium blankets to cure that arthritis?
- If your cough acts up, try a heroin-laced cough suppressant!
- Is your syphilis flaring up? Why not take some mercury?
- If you're having trouble losing weight, introduce a ten-foot long tapeworm into your digestive tract!

These ideas sound absolutely crazy to us. However, these are all real health fads from days gone by. At one point in time, the sheer popularity of these treatment options made them viable cures for a variety of medical ailments. You may think that we "modern people" have evolved past such silliness, but we haven't. Consider the millions of bottles of "vitamin water" we consume every year.

Despite being labeled as a "health drink" this product contains huge amounts of high-fructose corn syrup and dangerous chemicals. The "bandwagon fallacy" is a logical fallacy in which something is considered true or desirable just because it is popular. (This fallacy is also referred to as "argumentum ad populum".) While popular ideas <u>may</u> be true, many popular trends and ideas lack a scientific or logical foundation. Popularity does <u>not</u> indicate validity.

When you are trying to convince someone that a popular idea is accurate and reliable, you're committing the bandwagon fallacy. Regardless of how many people agree with your opinion or idea, it may still be utter nonsense. "Everyone's doing it", is no reason to do something; however, saying this is easier than making a rational argument and standing up for our own choices. I talked about heuristics earlier—our human mechanisms for creating cognitive rules of thumb that make processing our lives faster and easier. The "social proof" provided by many people engaging in an action or committing to an ideology has powerful influence over our choices. To simplify the complex decisions of daily life, we rely on social proof to help us choose appropriate actions. We humans like to see ourselves as independent thinkers; however, a wide spectrum of research has demonstrated that we look to <u>others</u> when we make decisions. We often ask:

Should I critically examine this situation or just follow the others?

Our attitude toward statistics also demonstrates the bandwagon fallacy. Consider the following statement: "If eighty percent of the population answers a question a certain way, this answer is correct." In many cases, the majority <u>will</u> be correct. Trusting the judgment of others is a fairly reliable metric for making decisions. However, many questions arise when we try to determine what a "majority" actually is:

- Are eighty percent of people truly selecting answer A?

- Was this a direct observation or an extrapolation?
- Would we consider fifty-one percent statistically significant enough to agree with a decision?
- What about the people who chose a different answer? Do they know something the others don't?

These questions must be addressed when we decide to follow the "bandwagon". Just because a belief is widely-held is no guarantee of its accuracy. This is where the fallacy lies.

We strengthen our beliefs through distorted biases and selectively pick information that fits those belief systems. This is called "confirmation bias"—we trust information that supports our beliefs and disregard information that conflicts with them. This "confirmation" gives further credence to our beliefs; with our beliefs strengthened, we will accept even more biased information as truth.

When an argument is based on the beliefs of a group of supposed experts, it carries a strong authoritative force. This "appeal to authority" persuades us to conform to an idea without thinking it through. Since childhood, we have grown up under the protective custody of authorities; parents and teachers have given us a simple framework for navigating complex social interactions: "Follow the rules and you'll be safe". Our tendency to trust authority figures carries on into our adult lives and manifests itself as a strong need to conform to symbols of authority. Bandwagon arguments that prominently display these symbols of authority put a tremendous amount of "pressure to conform" on audiences.

We humans respect old things. Somehow just "being old" or "having been done for a long time" gives an idea a measure of authority. For example, we revere and respect old, poorly-constructed, gas-guzzling cars when we see them on the highway—just because they're old. This is referred to as the "appeal to tradition".

The recent phenomenon of "going viral" is a great example of the bandwagon fallacy. Some of the videos that appear on my Facebook feed are absolutely ridiculous; however, I often end up watching them from start to finish. In the end, I feel thoroughly cheated out of my time. So—did I watch that video because it had ninety-thousand views—or am I actually interested in it?

Anything that attracts attention will attract more attention; people's interest in something is in itself interesting, generating a "snowball effect". Like a snowball rolling down a hill, it starts growing out-of-control. Before you know it, everyone is watching the same stupid video. This concept applies regardless of whether the information in a video is legitimate or a bunch of lies. A large view count alone is enough to get people to watch a video. This effect is known as the "Matthew Effect", a phrase coined by sociologist Robert K. Murton examining the culminative advantage of economic capital, or what has been more commonly describes as, "the rich getting richer and the poor getting poorer". In a nutshell, people often consider an idea's popularity to be a sign of its validity.

At this point, you may be thinking that you make your own informed decisions – that are in no way externally influenced by such superficialities such as popularity or "appeals to authority". However, if you honestly ask yourself why you prefer certain brands or subscribe to certain opinions, you may be surprised. An honest review of your motivations and logical decisions may reveal "argumentum ad populum" as the true reason for your choices.

The bandwagon fallacy also works through our need to display proper social etiquette. People respect social convention and fear appearing impolite or out-of-touch. Upon viewing what is the popular "opinion" or "decision", we fear offending those around us with potentially offensive ideas and opinions and instead succumb to the status quo. This tendency toward the status quo is reinforced by the rewarding feeling of aligning ourselves with others.

Well, what about the "haters"? The rebels? What about the people who don't want to engage in an activity just <u>because</u> everyone else is doing it?

Rebels may think they're rebels, but clever marketers influence them just like the rest of us. Saying, "Everyone is doing it" may turn some off some people from an idea. These people will look for alternatives, which (if cleverly planned) can be exactly what a marketer or persuader wants you to believe. If I want you to consider an idea, and know you vehemently reject popular opinion in favor of maintaining your independence and uniqueness, I would present the majority option first, which you would reject in favor of my actual preference. We are often tricked when we try to maintain a position of defiance. People use this reversal to make us "independently" choose an option which suits their purposes. A brand like Apple has taken full effect of our defiance towards the mainstream and positioned itself as a rebel; which has created even stronger brand loyalty.

In conclusion, the "appeal to authority" argument tricks us into believing arguments and ideas based solely on their popularity. Since childhood, popular ideas and thoughts have provided us with a social navigation system; this creates social cohesion in communities. However, when presented with arguments that the majority supports, we must think critically and ask ourselves if they are truly right. This is best summarized by Mark Twain, who said, "Whenever you find yourself on the side of the majority, it is time to pause and reflect".

Chapter 10:
False Cause

◆ ◆ ◆

"Correlation does not imply causation, but it does waggle its eyebrows suggestively and gesture furtively while mouthing, 'look over there'."

—xkcd catalog[xxix]

If I told you the total consumption of sour cream in the US was highly correlated to the number of motorcyclists killed in non-collision transport accidents, would you believe me? What if you were to discover the per capital consumption of chickens had a direct correlation to total US crude oil imports? An even more shocking example is the undeniable correlation of people who died after falling out of fishing boats and the marriage rate in Kentucky. If you want more of these websites check out a wonderful website by – Tyler Vigin.

Clearly, there must be some secret plot occurring throughout the US to arrange such highly similar correlations. Perhaps oil importers are eating only chicken at lunchtime or maybe people have been carelessly eating sour cream on the roads, spilling it everywhere and causing an startling increase in motorcycle accidents.

The above scenarios are all possible; however, the most likely situation is that these are all examples of "false cause". The false cause fallacy is also commonly referred to as "post hoc ergo propter hoc", which is Latin for "after this, therefore because of this".

In a complicated world, we search for meaning. Humans are naturally curious; we want to understand why events take place. When an event occurs, our brains search for possible causes and then usually pick one or two. These causes become our rationales for an event's occurrence.

Assigning causes to events is an important function of the human brain. Our brain is a giant-pattern-detection machine; it sorts and categorizes complex stimuli to make our human experience a more streamlined process. It examines new events based on their perceived danger, familiarity, and social context. Subscribing causality to current events helps our brains predict future events. If the cause of Event A was Reason B, then the next time we encounter a similar situation to Event A, we will predict Reason B to cause the same situation. This system usually serves us well; it evolved primarily to detect and assess potential threats. Stereotypes and judgments of character work in the same way: Bob was late to the meeting today, therefore Bob will be late to the next meeting. While this model has its flaws, it does help us predict future behavior; whether reliable or not.

The most powerful example of our need to ascribe meaning to an event is the confusion and shock caused by witnessing a horrific accident. When we witnesses a shocking accident that leads to serious injury or death, our first reaction is shock. We are shocked at what we just saw and look for reasons why the event occurred. Although we may have no idea of what really happened, that doesn't mean we can't make assumptions. Causality is rarely a product of thorough consideration—it is usually based on biased evidence. Regardless of how poor our evidence is (and the decisions we base on these assumptions), we have at least assigned casualty to the event. However, once we determine causality, changing this perception is quite difficult. The "false cause" fallacy relies on our coming to conclusions based <u>solely</u> on the <u>order of events</u>—and not taking into account other factors that might rule out this connection.

The truth is, the world is messy. We can't always understand why things happen. Sometimes, the cause of an event is so simple it escapes detection; other times, the causes are multifarious and not subject to direct observation. Whether we want to acknowledge it or not, randomness plays a big part in the occurrence of many events. We are not able to understand or observe the majority of the factors that influence events. Our human tendency to associate faulty incomplete evidence with a cause is one of the primary reasons why the scientific method is so important. The mantra that "correlation does not imply causation" refers to the idea that events that happen to coincide with other events are not necessarily related. The examples in this chapter are a testament to that. Naturally, chicken consumption doesn't cause the US to import more oil; these two trends are <u>statistically</u> related, but not <u>casually</u> related. We must take "confounding variables" into account; these variables are either coincidental or totally random. To prove something beyond any doubt requires the rigor of the scientific process.

When we want to convince people to agree with us in an argument, we rarely approach causality so fairly. We overemphasize one contributing variable and assume it's the sole cause of an event's occurrence. People don't like to admit they don't know things. There are a myriad of potential confounding factors. Our need to be correct and certain causes us to pick one reason and support that choice. Why admit you don't know something when you can just pick a reason and stick to it?

This need to be correct and stay correct often comes up when we speak with others about complicated social issues. Everyone has an opinion and we are all entitled to that right; however, the sad truth is that most of us are wrong—most of the time. Whether we want to admit it or not we don't know why most things happened. Event aren't caused by only one or two factors. However, we face a powerful contradiction when considering current events; we must either ignore confounding variables and examine a small subset of incomplete information—or admit we don't know enough to have an opinion on this subject. The social ramifications of the latter are much more severe. For example, if you hire a professional who indicates they don't know what they're talking about, you may appreciate their honesty; however, you would likely be displeased with their level of competence.

The idea that "correlation equals causation" is one of the primary forms of "evidence" for many believers in pseudoscience. Proponents of these theories often conflate correlation with causation to support their claims and don't test these casual relationships. They ignore confounding variables and promote one sole cause. Vitamin C is a poignant reminder of this fallacy. Vitamin C will not stop you from getting sick. The belief that taking massive amounts of Vitamin C when you're sick to expedite the process of recovery isn't supported by scientific evidence. If you don't take Vitamin C when you're sick, you'll just as fast as if you had. This is just one example of how promoters of pseudoscientific health fads make claims based on correlations — not actual evidence.

The false cause or "post hoc ergo propter hoc bias" affects everyone. If we don't regularly ask ourselves, "How certain am I?", we are bound to fall victim to this fallacy. In the wonderful words of Conservapedia (Wikipedia for conservatives) founder Andre Schlafly, *"In Romania, abortion was illegal under two decades of rule by the communist dictator Nicolae Ceausescu, and the country enjoyed one of the lowest breast cancer rates in the entire world during that time, far lower than comparable Western countries."* [xxx] The next time someone makes a claim about how effective or useful something is, make sure to exercise a little skepticism. As pattern recognition supercomputers, we humans are prone to picking up on <u>any</u> signals and correlating unrelated events.

Remember, just because two things occur at the same time doesn't mean they're related. A causal relationship can only be established after a thorough examination of the facts. Confounding variables make actually knowing what causes an event complicated (and in most cases, impossible). This raises an interesting philosophical question: If the true causal factors of events in life are often too difficult to understand, what is the majority of human understanding based on? If you were to break down all the statistical causes of an event, the resulting definition of causation would be too complex for the average person to understand. This leaves us with another question: "How much of what we know is actually confabulated lies, assumptions, and bad reasoning?"

Chapter 11:
Appeal to Emotion

♦ ♦ ♦

Karen: "Power lines cause cancer. I met a little boy with cancer who lived just 20 miles from a power line who looked into my eyes and said, in his weak voice, 'Please do whatever you can so that other kids won't have to go through what I am going through.' I urge you to vote for this bill to tear down all power lines and replace them with monkeys on treadmills."[xxxi]

If you want effective advertising, you might want to include a few of these themes: sexy scantily-clad women, children, cute animals, and barbaric violence. Any of these will trigger emotional reactions that can effectively turn off people's rational-thinking processes. Instead of thinking clearly, we react emotionally. When people try to win arguments or defeat an opponent using emotional reactions, they are guilty of the "appeal to emotion" fallacy.

This technique is one of the more basic forms of argument; however, it's still extremely effective. Appeals to emotion play on listeners' stereotypes and prejudices, effectively short-cutting any logical assessments of the matters at hand. These arguments appeal to emotions like fear, hatred, pity, pride, and envy. When emotions replace logic, the facts are unimportant; proving yourself correct becomes monumentally more important. I'm sure we've all engaged in a frustrating conversation-turned-argument in which we experienced escalating levels of anger and frustration. This often reaches a point where we forget what we were arguing about. When someone "pushes our buttons", we react emotionally; we say or do things that an otherwise rational evaluation would discourage.

When we shift into this "argument mode", any need for facts and evidence goes out the window. Instead, we use persuasive language to entice people into an emotional dance with us - and the subject matter. Words and ideas can touch upon hidden fears and pain spots. Upon experiencing these visceral feelings, not only are our logical faculties suspended, we also begin to think the statements we're hearing are true. How can an argument causing such powerful emotions be false? We take our emotions as a form of evidence; emotions <u>feel</u> valid and reliable, though they rarely are. Ironically, we can offer no substantial proof of this—and often accept arguments with wholly invalid premises.

I can't stress the power of the appeal to emotion enough. An adequately-powerful emotional appeal turns your brain off and hypnotizes you into conformity. Perhaps this sounds slightly hyperbolic, but the appeal to emotion has been the primary method of mass propaganda for the last century. Since antiquity, philosophers have warned of the power of emotions. Like two explosive substances, they should not be mixed. Seneca warned that *"Reason herself, to whom the reins of power have been entrusted, remains mistress only so long as she is kept apart from the passions".*[xxxii]

The ability of emotions to make our minds inclined to act irrationally was also mentioned by Aristotle, "The orator persuades by means of his hearers, when they are roused to emotion by his speech; for the judgments we deliver are not the same when we are influenced by joy or sorrow, love or hate".[xxxiii] However, ancient philosophers weren't the only ones aware of the mind-bending power of emotional appeals. The father of modern public relations, Edward Bernays, championed the use of emotional appeals to change the attitudes of the masses. Messages that contain "loaded information" target the fears, impulses, and habits of the masses; those that wield them use powerful emotional currents to achieve radical change. Bernays claimed, "In certain cases, we can effect some change in public opinion with a fair degree of accuracy by operating a certain mechanism, just as a motorist can regulate the speed of his car by manipulating the flow of gasoline."[xxxiv] This idea has been experimented and expanded on by some of the most notorious manipulators of public opinion—from Hitler to today's Islamic fundamentalists—to capture their supporters emotions and demonize their opponents.

When a brain that evolved to make split-second decisions while hunting, foraging, and trying to survive is faced with a new situation, it makes the most cognitively-undemanding decision. We are biased towards our emotions over rational analysis. Rational thinking must be taught in school and cultivated over a lifetime of good habits and daily reminders. Unfortunately, we don't carry these little "fortune cookies" of rational reminders around with us. Like a six-hundred-pound bull colliding with an average man, reason stands no chance against emotion.

When we want to convince someone of something, appealing to their emotions is a more effective path than using a rational argument. Ideally, we should all pursue good arguments based on solid premises followed by valid conclusions; however, rarely are we afforded such a luxury. When it comes to important issues, people are already emotionally primed. It is quite difficult to cool off your emotionally-primed brain and favor a more reasonable argument.

Approaching issues of emotional importance with rational arguments is a waste of time. Rarely can we connect with and convince someone to agree with us who has made an emotional commitment to another idea. For this reason, manipulating emotions is the most powerful way to shape attitudes. Words loaded with latent meanings and connotations that depict individuals, groups, or ideas from a biased-emotional perspective steer listeners' minds in a desired direction. This path is subtle; many people don't notice it at all. When information is wrapped in emotionally-charged messages it slips into people's minds without their awareness. Emotions provide a ladder on which we can overcome a person's rational walls of protection and slip unnoticed into their mind to plant the seed of an idea.

A good emotional argument is so powerful it can actually change our behavior. We rarely think of emotions as originating externally; rather, we view our experiences as internally-generated. When we adopt this "internally-generated emotions" model, any subsequent feelings we have modify our belief systems. If you are subject to a powerful appeal to emotion, your mind treats the emotions you feel are as a form of evidence. This evidence is taken as "how we actually feel" about a subject. We then change our beliefs about that subject or situation to match our emotions. In short, people match their beliefs to their emotions.

When we make emotional appeals, we rarely use positive emotions; negative emotions are much more useful. Framing arguments in terms of loss, pain, and fear really gets peoples' attention. When we think about stressful negative situations, we activate a very different circuitry in the brain than when we think positively. Intense emotional pressure deceases our performance quality—on even the simplest tasks. Modern psychology has verified this assumption with a multitude of experiments. In Nobel Prize winning researcher Daniel Kahneman's book, *Thinking Fast and Slow*, he describes two pathways the brain utilizes to form thoughts and process information:

Pathway 1: Emotional, stereotypical, subconscious, entirely automatic, and extremely fast

Pathway 2: Logical, calculating, considering, conscious, effortful, and slow

Emotional appeals side with pathway one; they provide instant answers to problems or situations. These answers are not logically or consciously processed. They often form the bulk of our "everyday" opinions. Research has shown that over a wide spectrum of tasks, people opt to make faster decisions—in an effort to save mental energy. Emotional appeals function solely on pathway number one: the highway to bad social decisions.

Messages and arguments that inspire fear work marvelously at making people pay attention. This "hyper focus" results from their not considering other variables. Focusing too much on a singular aspect of an event or situation impairs our ability to make logical decisions. Messages that make people feel guilty encourage them to reevaluate their beliefs and behaviors. The emotion of guilt occurs when our behaviors don't conform to our internalized ethical, religious, or moral standards. By experiencing guilt though an argument, we feel required to change our belief systems or behaviors to alleviate it.

The most obvious appeal to emotions is anger. Anger is also the clearest example of "pathway number one". Feeling guilty about "overreacting" to a certain event is a result of an ultra-fast "pathway one" response. We are not given time to use our logic; we find ourselves responding before we can even assess what's happening.

Not all appeals are negative; positive appeals can also function incredibly well. Appeals to compassion and pride also skew people's judgment. Images or concepts that elicit emotionally compassionate responses spur us into actions we might not otherwise take. This isn't always a bad thing; however, it can be easily used to manipulate us. When we experience shocking images, we respond instinctually; our brains bypasses our "logical analysis circuits". This feeling is heightened if we see the person experiencing a negative event as similar to us. We give "similar people" preference over "dissimilar people". We do not give arguments that contain graphic depictions of death, injury, or injustice rational assessments; instead, we are shocked into biased decision-making.

When visual cues are focused on one individual person, this effect is often greatly exaggerated. We don't give Problems involving <u>many</u> people the same priority things that happen to just <u>one</u> person. Noted researcher Dan Ariely states, *"In many ways, it is very sad that the only effective way to get people to respond to suffering is through an emotional appeal, rather than through an objective reading of massive need. The upside is that when our emotions are awakened, we can be tremendously caring. Once we attach an individual face to suffering, we're much more willing to help, and we go far beyond what economists would expect from rational, selfish, maximizing agents."*[xxxv]

The emotion of pride functions similarly to compassion. Arguments or appeals to your pride motivate you to complete tasks and engage in actions; these often involve respect, admiration, or acquisition of status symbols. While not often discusses, pride is a powerful motivator of human behavior. When carefully embedded into an argument, it works very well. However, researchers have shown that appeals to pride operate differently in various cultures. Collectivist cultures responded better to pride-based appeals whereas individualistic countries respond more favorably to empathy-based appeals.[xxxvi]

In the 2002 book, *Art, Argument, and Advocacy: Mastering Parliamentary Debate*, writers Kate Shuster and John Meany mention one of the most common emotion-loaded phrases: "think of the children".[xxxvii] They concluded that the use of such a phrase in an argument is a logical fallacy that appeals to emotions. This phrase triggers emotional thinking in people that circumnavigates logic. Shuster and Meany offered this example: *"I know this national missile defense has its detractors, but won't someone please think of the children?"*[xxxviii]

The next time someone attempts to end a discussion by issuing an unanswerable argument and appealing to your emotions – think about what's <u>really</u> happening. Appeals to emotion follow the faster, emotion-based pathway in our brain to create emotionally-based reactions, opinions, and ideas—not logical ones. Instead, follow the pathway that rational humans like you and I want to follow – pathway number two.

Chapter 12:
Argument from Ignorance

♦ ♦ ♦

Sia: "The Nighttime Bacon Monster has been terrorizing the residents of my city for over ten years. The creature awakens in the middle of the night to consume all of the bacon within a three-or-four house vicinity. Whether cooked or uncooked, it devours it all.

You can't prove the Nighttime Bacon Monster doesn't exist. However, you also can't prove it's a fake, as its continued existence evades all scientific endeavors to document and locate it. Therefore, based on these failed attempts, the Nighttime Bacon Monster must be real."

I hope such a terrible creature doesn't exist. It would deprive me not only of my bacon, but also my joy in the mornings. This story includes an "appeal to ignorance" (or the "appeal to incredulity"). Stating that something is true simply because it hasn't been shown to be false—or that something is false because it hasn't been proved true—is a logical fallacy. A lack of imagination on the listeners' part implies there must be some semblance of truth hidden within the argument.

The argument from ignorance presents an interesting problem: it employs a "false dichotomy" and the "burden of proof" fallacy. If an argument is presented and people must choose to either support it or refute it, we exclude the possibility of a third option—insufficient evidence. Arguments of a complex nature aren't so easily defined; assigning causality is a tricky business. An argument may be true, false, undetermined between the two, or just unknowable.

When we present someone with the argument from ignorance, we also shift the burden of proof. Since I have already claimed the Nighttime Bacon Monster exists, you must disprove its existence. Making a claim puts me on argumentative high ground for two reasons: First, since I've made a ridiculous claim you feel the need to refute it. Second, you are unable to refute it because my argument is essentially flawed. However, I can frame your inability to refute my argument as a demonstration of my argument's superiority and validity. Basically, since you can't prove me wrong—I must be right!

You can see the cruel twist in logic here—but don't be fooled. You're reading this book right now using your mind's "logical and rational analysis circuits"; however, we often don't use these faculties when we encounter this argument in our daily lives.

Argument from ignorance is often used by creationists, who hold up an extremely complicated aspect of biology as solid proof of a creator. Evolution has been studied thoroughly but there are still areas of knowledge to explore. For example, no non-design explanation explains the development of certain organs. This has taken as a sign of the validity of creationism. People say that if science is unable to explain why something is untrue, it must be true. When an inability to refute an argument presents itself, any claim can suffice, regardless of its lack of supporting evidence. Again, we see the same theme; our deep, human need to feel certain—even in the face of ignorance.

The need to find causes in the world is hard-wired into our brains. From simple sounds in the night to the diseases and struggles that afflict mankind worldwide, we all love to seek explanations. Early humans exemplify this perfectly with their mythical worlds of supernatural entities. Inexplicable events were considered to be the actions of superhuman forces beyond the realm of regular understanding—which needed to be revered. As the art of science slowly began to develop, people abandoned these naturalistic explanations in favor of a simpler scientific model. Which each advancement in science, these stories have been relegated one-by-one to the status of myths, superstitions, and fairy tales. As each of these gaps-in-understanding are filled in by scientific knowledge, our reliance on deities and supernatural powers grows ever smaller.

Arguments from ignorance can flourish within these gaps. The only difference is that now science has advanced to the point where we can explain away most of these silly arguments thoroughly and effectively. Steven Fry summarizes it best, *"Astrologers will tell you things like: Science doesn't know everything." Well, of course science doesn't know everything. But because science doesn't know everything, that doesn't mean science knows nothing. Science knows enough for us to be watched by a few million people now on television, for these lights to be working, for quite extraordinary miracles to have taken place in terms of the harnessing of the physical world and our dim approaches towards understanding it."* [xxxix]

Sometimes, people use valid arguments to prove a point

is wrong—but fail terribly. When a person tries to discredit science by stating a scientific principle, they are attempting to use logic to refute an otherwise solid claim. An excellent example of this is author and TV commentator Bill O'Reilly's declaration that ocean tides are an unexplained phenomenon. He claimed that since ocean tides were unexplained, a divine force must have willed the oceans to move. Anyone with more than a sixth-grade science education can see the massive gap in Mr. O'Reilly's logic. However, when it comes to phenomenon we can't explain—or are too lazy to find an answer for—the best way to fill in those gaps is to posit an argument that is either beyond the scope of knowledge or simply too difficult to prove wrong.

The argument of ignorance contributes to "wishful thinking". Hope and positive beliefs about the future are essential to our motivation, focus, and pursuit of goals. However, there is a fine line beyond which out hopes drag us into a land of unreality. When causality can't be logically assigned, we opt for a wishful system of thinking. Similar to the previous idea of "gaps", we forecast that an assumed causal fact will reoccur if the circumstances are right. If it's nighttime and we haven't removed the bacon from the fridge, the Nighttime Bacon Monster will surely strike. This hypothesis is used to predict future events; however, it is entirely based on a lack of evidence and proof.

The appeal to ignorance works in a deceptive way. We must be wary of arguments that implement this approach as they try to give us the logical "runaround". If I state that an argument is true, your inability to refute it (or the weakness of your refuting argument) can be taken as evidence of my argument's superiority. However, this isn't accurate—your ignorance isn't proof of my knowledge.

A mature, rational person must be able to freely admit, "I don't know". If we fail to do this, we are stuck believing in a world where we invent "gaps" in our thinking. Worse yet, we can selectively ignore contradictions to appear correct. Hippocrates spoke of this dilemma, *"People think that epilepsy is divine simply because they don't have any idea what causes epilepsy. But I believe that someday we will understand what causes epilepsy, and at that moment, we will cease to believe that it's divine. And so it is with everything in the universe."*

Chapter 13:
Special Pleading

♦ ♦ ♦

A magician claims to have these powers: levitation, making all manner of objects disappear mysteriously, and turning golf balls into baby chickens. However, when confronted by a skeptical TV reporter, the magician is unable to perform any of his tricks. He is unable to produce even one baby chicken. The magician tells the reporter that since he brought a TV camera along, his magic wouldn't work.

In a 2009 soccer game, Danish goalkeeper Kim Christensen was exposed on camera moving the opposing team's goalposts. This video footage showed him purposely widening the goalposts. Luckily, Christensen's little goalpost trick was noticed by a keen referee twenty minutes into the game. The idea of modifying standards of judgment in order to gain an advantage is called "special pleading". Special pleading works by asking or creating an exception to the rule. This exception is applied to a specific case that claims to be different from the standard. While this is applicable in some cases, it becomes a fallacy when unjustified. To avoid appearing incorrect, we attempt to qualify our situation as somehow different from the established standards of rational assessment. We don't want to admit we're wrong; instead, we post-rationalize our decisions.

When faced with a situation in which we are totally wrong, we are faced with two decisions. First, we can avoid dealing with the situation by ignoring the problem and the opposing argument. Second, we can change what we believe in order to maintain a defensive position. In order for a faulty argument to work, we need a way to present a logical inconsistency or a contradiction. What better way to do this than to propose a special circumstance that makes our position or argument special?

The majority of us aren't idiots; we maintain a rational standard to assess the validity and strength of arguments. We may even refute or look down on ideas that lack a solid premise. When we encounter a situation that falls under the purview of established standards, we remain consistent with our belief systems and judge it accordingly. Having a steady reliable system of socially enforced standards is essential for living a consistent life. If we were to decide on a new set of standards for each situation, we would be mentally exhausted. We rely on standards for judgment that don't assess each case based on its idiosyncrasies.

When we are restricted by our criteria, we are forced to declare our own situation as "special"—regardless of the evidence. This accomplishes two important functions: it keeps us from appearing wrong and maintains the consistency we need to keep us feeling good about ourselves. There is a little part inside all of us that thinks we are special. Perhaps this came from our parents, too many politically-correct messages, or pop culture. However, regardless of where it came from, our subjective experience of reality makes us feel unique and distinct from others. This feeling of "specialness" translates into the idea of privileged exceptions from rational judgment; we do things we would not accept in others. "Moving the goalposts" is the method we use to accomplish this feat.

The things we find undesirable can be easily persecuted; yet, we reserve special justification for the ideas we support. Whether this support is our own decision, or a result of cultural training, the result is the same: the exceptions we make for certain arguments are definitely not made on a logical foundation. Consider drugs and alcohol, two killers that create an immense amount of death and misery. Logic would dictate that the enormous medical and human costs of these substances would see them banned immediately. However, this is not the case; instead, society puts the full force of the law into fighting comparatively benign drugs such as marijuana. Their position is that anything stronger than alcohol and tobacco is not acceptable. This is illogical special pleading at its finest; though alcohol and tobacco don't get you "high", they slowly and systematically destroy your body. For some reason, these drugs are more acceptable than others.

Proponents of Biblical morality are experts at special pleading. Biblical literalists (who claim that morality can only come from the Bible) are happy to follow some rules, but not others. If the Bible provides such clear moral instructions why are only some parts applicable? Why is gay and lesbian discrimination justified by the Bible when stoning disobedient children, selling slaves, and overall brutality are considered unacceptable? If biblical texts provide the sole source of moral instruction, surely I could punish those naughty neighborhood children with a good-old fashioned stoning, right?

Special pleading gives us an "out" from terrible arguments. We avoid feeling inconsistent with our value systems and create realities in which our actions are justified and acceptable. We do this to accomplish one important mission—feeling "correct". The next time someone says their case is "special", pause and consider whether such a claim qualifies a departure from rational discourse. We may be convinced of our "specialness" in our own minds; however, reality doesn't consider us unique. We must take responsibility for our illogical actions and learn from them. Our failure to do so perpetuates an endless cycle of dumb decisions and willful ignorance. Don't be dumb. Admit you're wrong when you are.

Chapter 14:
Appeal to Authority

♦ ♦ ♦

As you look up at the racks of cigarettes you see an eye-catching package of cigarettes. You look on the red packaging and see the words, "Physicians Trust Lucky". You think to yourself, "These must be good cigarettes. Doctors like them and doctors know lots of things.

From the time we were little, we have been taught to place our trust in authority figures like parents, teachers, and policeman. Children grow up with these figures watching over and protecting them. The majority of us (some trouble-makers aside) confer complete trust in the people that play these social roles. As we get older, we encounter other forms of authority in the workplace. Authority provides us with an easy and effective way of navigating the social landscape. It makes the world easier to understand, predict, and evaluate. By following the guidance of experts and authority figures we use their knowledge to give us a better understanding. By leveraging another person's knowledge, we have the ability to try our new actions with confidence.

Symbols of authority confer power on people. If a man

dressed in formal clothing said you couldn't do something, you will be more likely to comply than if he were wearing regular clothing. Our tendency to trust authority figures is so great that it make us vulnerable to a form of fallacious reasoning. The "argument from authority" states that ideas supported by authority figures are accurate, reliable, and shouldn't be second-guessed.

This fallacy works in two ways: First, an argument can be grounded in an authoritative source whose opinions are true and scientifically valid. Second, an argument can be grounded in non-authoritative forms whose arguments may or may not be true. Personal bias, lack of evidence, and being a non-expert all constitute this non-authoritative form. Think about how much respect we give to people we see as experts. Slap a couple of letters after your name and your opinion will be more highly regarded by others. People rarely stop and ask to see proof of authority. To do so would be rude and socially inappropriate. We take markers and symbols of authority as evidence of people's credibility.

When we interact with others through an anonymous medium like the Internet, we cannot properly assess who people are; we open ourselves up to manipulation. When encountering a form of authority, our brains revert to a childlike automatic mode of processing; we don't consider the validity of the information we receive. If someone uses an Albert Einstein quote about "energy" to support their beliefs or claims, this doesn't validate their idea. Quotes taken out of context can be used to support or dismiss any arguments. Quotes from authority figures who speak out of their fields are of limited use; they do have some slight credence because this person is respected, knowledgeable, and intelligent.

We can even use ourselves as a source of authority. Have you ever heard someone say something like, "I know myself and I would never do that"? Using yourself as a form of authority is called "Ipse dixit" in Latin. In reality, you don't know how a future hypothetical situation will unfold. Self-awareness doesn't give you psychic powers to decide in advance how an event will play out. Quotes from authority figures are often used out of context. Just because you cite a highly-respected figure doesn't mean your argument isn't terrible. I could say something absolutely ridiculous and find a supporting out-of-context quote. This "argument of veneration" assumes that if an authority source said something, it must be true. This idea has been taken to an extreme with Internet memes. These viral images display a prominent figure with associated text, usually agreeing or disagreeing with an idea. This conflation of authority figures with things they would probably never say creates an amusing play on the argument from authority fallacy.

I'm not insinuating that experts shouldn't be believed; however, I am suggesting that we should better evaluate our sources. If I am famous, does that somehow give my opinion more credence? I would hope not. However, when we think fast we rarely make such delineations. A person may be an absolute genius in one regard but totally ignorant in another field. However, unless this discrepancy is large we usually don't notice it. For example, if a Nobel Prize-winning cellular biologist offered advice about basketball, no one would pay much attention. But what if that same cell biologist provided advice about HIV prevention? Wouldn't you listen carefully? This person's opinion within the realm of biology would be highly respected by many. The problem is that—even within one field of science—many specializations exist.

In the late 1980s, this exact scenario occurred: Peter Duesberg, a revered cell biologist, claimed that AIDS was caused by recreational drug use. Despite overwhelming later evidence that HIV was the sole cause of AIDS, Duesberg stuck to his position. Peter Duesberg is still widely cited by HIV denialists (yes, this fringe group actually exists). Expert knowledge is important, but only within the context of what they are actually an "expert" on. Making assumptions and asserting personal opinions without scientific evidence (even in you're a seemingly-smart person) is an abandonment of your personal responsibility to investigate the truth.

When claims are not tested, we can fall victim to falsehoods that can perpetuate themselves far into the future. Take the "tongue map" for example. Do you remember this thing? It was a multicolored map of the human tongue indicating the different areas of the tongue associated with each taste. In actuality, the tongue map was actually a mistake from a translated German document. However, this didn't stop it from being used in textbooks and taught to students for the next eighty years. Despite the fact that this theory could have easily been proven wrong by putting a piece of candy anywhere on your tongue and still finding it sweet, it persisted. Backed by the weight of authoritative evidence, educators didn't even bother to challenge the tongue map.

Appeals to authority are often created by using a regular person. The idea of using regular people as a form of authority is a powerful form of marketing. Testimonials achieve this by having regular folks support a product or idea. The idea works along this principle: "Hey! I'm average, and you are too! Therefore, you should support my average claim." We like people who are similar to us; the "average person" is very relatable.

The appeal to authority technique has been widely use by marketers. The common-cold-preventing medicine, Airborne, was said to be "invented by a schoolteacher". Despite the fact that the formula was nothing more than some low-quality vitamins mixed that fizzed when put into water, it still sold like crazy. The narrative of a secret formula discovered by a simple schoolteacher somehow made it more believable. (The company that made Airborne was later sued for millions for deceiving customers.) Conspiracy theorists love the appeal to authority approach. They often believe experts cannot be trusted because they are "part of the system". Instead, they give too much credence to "regular people's" accounts of events.

We can see social evidence of the appeal to authority principle in daily conversation. A perpetual name-dropper does this to align with a perceived source of authority and add credibility and status to their opinions and ideas. Mentioning important people or institutions within a casual context is sometimes referred to as the "false authority" fallacy. The next time someone "name-drops" , remember this is an attempt to convince you either of the validity of an argument—or of their own worth.

Dropping names can overwhelm you; you may feel compelled to comply to a request or support a cause. On October 4th 1914, the "Manifesto of the Ninety-Three" was released. This was a proclamation of ninety-three of German's greatest scientists, scholars, and artists; it provided absolute support for the German government's military actions. Whether the members of the intelligentsia that signed this manifesto were coerced into doing so or not remains a mystery. However, the manifesto galvanized German support for the war effort. The authoritative-social proof displayed by those ninety-three names exerted enormous pressure on average citizens to comply.

The modern equivalent of this is the "expert for hire". These people make substantial incomes by providing companies and organizations with testimonials supporting certain causes. These "rent-a-quote" experts are used widely in commercial enterprises and legal situations. Experts like these are often paid by attorneys to provide "professional" opinions in court. The problem is, the credentials of "expert witnesses" are rarely tested. People mistakenly believe that a high level of education qualifies people to comment on fields they know nothing about. This "credential bullying" has become widespread as the number of institutions offering high-level diplomas has dramatically increased in recent years.

Not all appeals to authority come from a man in a suit with a fancy title. Being "old" can just as easily elevate an idea to a status of authority. This is referred to as the "appeal of ancient wisdom"; it has become a hallmark of bad logic. This appeal also manifests itself in a few other biases; the most obvious is the "appeal to tradition". A long cultural tradition of ineffectual logic and pseudoscience doesn't make an idea more valid. Stupid ideas can be perpetuated far into the future. I described this earlier in relation to the anecdotal evidence fallacy. Only with science and critical thinking can we to determine what's reasonable and valid. The age of a practice or idea doesn't determine its credibility.

Think of all the ideas that were once widely accepted— the majority of these have long since been abandoned and discarded. However, each one of these transitions took time. The ancient practice of trepanation (drilling holes in your skull) existed for hundreds of years until it was thoroughly abandoned. Homeopathy is a more extreme example of "new age" medicine that claims to use ancient untested substances to alleviate a variety of illnesses. Despite the fact that there is some evidence showing ancient foods and medicines can actually help, this doesn't vindicate the ancient-wisdom-is-best idea. The ancients who discovered traditional sources of medicine often did so by trial-and-error; these accidental discoveries were further promoted by wishful thinking and supernatural beliefs. The trial-and-error method is only valid if followed by a thorough scientific evaluation. Willow tree bark is an example of this. This pain-relieving substance is the principle ingredient in aspirin. Ancient people found this substance through the trial-and-error method, but it was verified through scientific research.

Appeals to authority through ancient practices can delude us into believing in nonsensical events or superstitions. The apocalypse predicted for 2012 9based on the Mayan Calendar) is a wonderful example of this. Some people believed a "doomsday" would occur on 21/12/12 despite the fact that this calendar doesn't work in the way they claimed. The validity provided by the "old" and "mystical" nature of this calendar was enough to encourage some people to believe in this "end of days". This fallacy also often arises with Chinese medicine and other herbal remedies—especially when salespeople claim a treatment is thousands of years old. In some people, this language sparks a sense of respect and admiration. They think, "Something that old must have been remarkably effective to persist into the modern era." However, ask yourself—was it the validity of this practice or people's stubborn belief in it that made it persist?

Only when you apply rational thinking can you depart from this need to <u>know</u> and <u>be right</u>. If you want to live truthfully, you must closely examine your beliefs. An wonderful example of ancient bullshit comes to us from the days of Plutarch and Ptolemy: some ancients believed garlic would destroy magnets. Unsurprisingly, when Sir Thomas Browne[xl] actually tried it out, he found it was complete nonsense. Science demands you actually experiment with things before making claims about their causality. Clearly, ancient people didn't have access to enough garlic, magnets, or curiosity—either that, or they had some kind of garlic we don't have now.

The appeal to authority is ingrained in us from childhood. We are raised under the protection and tutelage of authority figures; however, as adults, we must examine this relationship. A blind deference to authority symbols can evoke this logical fallacy. People use the appeal to authority and symbols such as professions, titles, wealth, lifespans, and popularity to validate their ideas. Arguments based on authority are not strong; a person who claims to be an expert may lack sufficient knowledge or experience in that field. Look for arguments that deal directly with evidence. The next time you encounter an authority who supports an idea, be critical. Ask yourself, "Am I judging this on evidence alone or being influenced by authority?"

This need for this clarity was captured beautifully by the Dalai Lama, "The ultimate authority must always rest with the individual's own reason and critical analysis".

Chapter 15:
Begging the Question

♦ ♦ ♦

"Why is Bob so dumb?"

Is he dumb? I don't know. But this question assumes he is. Its premise is based on Bob's stupidity. This is an example of circular reasoning—also known as "begging the question". When you beg the question, the premise is included in the claim. By asking people "why" Bob is so dumb; the premise of his "dumbness" is established. This question forces people into focusing on the "why" without an examination of the premises. Assuming this premise to be true doesn't qualify as evidence for the conclusion. Begging the question originates from a Latin phrase, "petito principiee", which means "assuming the initial point". This is exactly what we are doing when we beg the question; we assume the premise to be true.

This kind of logic is referred to as "circular logic" because the explanation of an event is basically the same as the event itself. For example, "Happiness is the highest good for a human being, since all other values are inferior to it." xli While happiness is clearly important, stating that happiness is the highest good contaminates the conclusion—that all other values are inferior to it. If this premise is not true, we are led down a potentially inaccurate path.

If I were to say, "Water will make you wet; if you jump into water, you will get wet", I would be offering a solid premise. When discussing a topic, it's imperative to start with a known and then (and only then) determine an unknown. When we beg the question we do the opposite; we start with a known and end up with an "equally known". We're just running in circles. Some people love to do this as a method of show others how correct they are; unfortunately, it's just *terrible* logic.

To avoid going down the rabbit-hole of epistemology, we will avoid examining circular logic in all of its nuances. It is important, however, to understand why people use such faulty logic. Most people guilty of this logical fallacy aren't aware of it. Rarely do we fully examine the premises we have accepted; instead, we take our belief systems for granted. When you believe an idea for a long time, it becomes thoroughly internalized. We don't subject internalized beliefs to the same rational evaluation as other ideas. We base our understandings of the world on internalized belief structures of causality that give us clarity and simplicity. For this reason, arguments afflicted with this fallacy are often incurable; they will persist until we bring them under the scrutiny of interpersonal inspection. When we believe our own nonsense to such a degree that we can't see through it, we may be subject to another problem, as well—denial.

There are two ways to feel better about ourselves: First, we can work hard and actually succeed. Second, we can systematically lie to ourselves. Unfortunately, we often choose the later. It's a lot easier to ignore our problems, faults, and issues than it is to face them directly. Upon honest reflection, we may all find we spend a significant portion of our lives in denial about ourselves. This often manifests as coping mechanisms for problems or issues we either don't want to deal with or deem too complicated. Denial is a disconnection from reality; however, it is an effective strategy. We talked earlier about the essential roles cognitive biases and logical fallacies play in our lives—they provide mental shortcuts. Denial is one of these shortcuts. By selectively focusing on what we want or don't want, we can selectively "create" our realities. We have been taught that problems our won't "go away" if we ignore them; however, this only happens when we know we have a problem. When we don't know something exists, there's no need to ignore it!

Let's look at some further examples of begging the question. Consider this statement: "Paranormal phenomena exist because I have had experiences which can only be described as paranormal". Remember, begging the question implies a stated premise is already true regardless of evidence. The premise here is that this person has had a paranormal experience; therefore, paranormal experiences must exist. However, this is based on the idea that his experiences were actually paranormal, which has not in any way been substantiated.

To understand this a little better, I will discuss "warranted" and "unwarranted" assumptions. Warranted assumptions are assumptions that are known to be true or which can be reasonably assumed to be true without required proof. For example: "Fire is hot", and "Tigers will eat you" are both excellent warranted assumptions, hardly anyone would deny either of these statements. On the other hand, unwarranted assumptions occur when an assumption *"is one that is controversial and one for which there is no general consensus among a vast majority of those with the appropriate knowledge or experience"*[xlii] A claim that seems unlikely or unreasonable requires proof. A claim doesn't become questionable simply because you or I question it—otherwise, every claim would be questionable. You don't need to prove everything you say; however, when you make unwarranted assumptions evidence is required, NOT assumed premises. As Carl Sagan once said, "Extraordinary claims require extraordinary evidence".

Let's examine another argument like this:

"Past-life memories of children prove that past lives exist because the children could have no other source for their memories besides having lived in the past."[xliii]

The premise here, that past lives exist, is assumed. The result, that children's memories are a result of past lives, is used as evidence to support this premise. However, this is the only source of information for this claim. The arguer should explain his position on past lives existing before making further assumed claims. This is an unwarranted claim.

Begging the question comes up all the time. Think about using the dictionary. Have you ever looked up a word only to see it defined by its synonyms? When part of a definition assumes a prior understanding of the term being defined, we run into this kind of circular definition. Another similar linguistic device is a "tautology". Tautologies are statements that works via the virtue of logic alone. Consider these examples: "The brown donkey is brown"; "In my opinion, I think that..." Both of these statements contain no useful information and are self-referential. You don't need to say "I think" when stating your opinion!

Another more salient example of a tautology is the catch-22. A catch-22 is a paradoxical situation from which an individual cannot escape due to contradictory rules. Try this:

- A Belgian law for foreigner laborers: If you want a work permit, you need a job. You can't get a job if you don't have a work permit.
- I got letter from the city threatening a fine if I didn't cut down tree on my property. I checked with the county; they threatened to fine me if I cut down this tree because it belongs to a protected species.

The term "catch-22" was originally coined by Joseph Heller in his 1961 novel, *Catch-22*. He described the absurd bureaucratic constraints placed on World War 2 soldiers. Similar to the above examples, a catch-22 occurs when you encounter rules, regulations, or procedures that you must abide by—but cannot dispute. Disputing these rules would be "against the rules". As you can see in the first example regarding work permits, a person often requires something that can only be had by <u>not</u> needing it. A catch-22 functions via faulty premises that trap you; this is similar to begging the question. A catch-22 is a social example of begging the question gone seriously wrong.

The next time you encounter an argument, stop and think about its premises. Are they warranted or unwarranted? If we aren't aware of this step, we can become easily bamboozled by arguments based on factious premises. More importantly, the begging the question fallacy gives us a glimpse into our own innate need to form self-serving beliefs. Belief structures are often held together by denial and our avoidance of examination. By avoiding problems or structuring our causal understandings of them on faulty or incomplete premises, we create self-serving conclusions. Ask yourself, "Is what I'm assuming based on evidence or assumption?"

Chapter 16:
Appeal to Nature

◆ ◆ ◆

Just because it came from the Earth doesn't mean it's healthy or good for you. Arsenic is also a naturally occurring substance. Who wants some arsenic? Don't worry. It's organic.

Terms like "organic", "natural", "nature-made", or "whole food" have all become synonymous with health. As our "diseases of civilization" increase, so does our obsession with health. As we grow more detached from a traditional way of life that included real food, regular exercise, and manageable levels of stress, we look for quick alternatives. Today, arguments for the "naturalness" of products, treatments, or therapies are constantly shoved into our faces. This is the "appeal to nature" fallacy. Just because something is natural doesn't mean it is healthy or good for us. Arsenic, sharks, jellyfish, and hundreds of poisons and toxics are all natural; however, they definitely aren't good for us. The word "natural" is a nebulous term that can be used without any context or credentials. Just because the Doritos chips in the local convenience store indicate they are made from natural ingredients and organic corn doesn't qualify them as a healthy snack. The word "natural" has no definition and can be used whenever it fits an argument.

The term "natural" begs the question. If I were to say product A is natural, and therefore, consumption of product A is a healthy choice, I am begging the question. This premise is not based on evidence, but assumption— how do I know this particular *natural* quality is legitimate? Think of how you feel when you hear a product is natural. The term itself is a "loaded term"— meaning it contains a latent meaning.

The natural fallacy often appears when we engage in discussions about food or health products. Supporters of the "all-natural approach" castigate "big pharma" and artificial chemicals. Arguments for an all-natural treatment for illnesses often lack research-based scientific evidence. Take the heart medication digoxin, for example; a natural product of the foxglove plant, it's an extremely poisonous plant. It is so poisonous, in fact, that it was serial killer Charles Cullen's murder weapon of choice. The foxglove plant is a great example of the blurred line between "natural" and "non-natural" treatments; it illustrates an important point: medical treatments are too complicated to be simply classified as "good" or "bad". The foxglove plant, when chemically extracted and dispensed as a pill can relieve heart arrhythmias. However, if this dosage is increased by just a little too much, it causes fatal heart arrhythmia. The question is—is foxglove good or bad? Natural substances contain hundreds (if not thousands) of compounds the work together in many ways. These interactions and effects are complicated and cannot be defined simply through the "natural-or-unnatural" dichotomy.

If this seems too abstract, think again of our need to simplify the world. Instead of a world of uncertainty, we seek one of clear causality and understandability. The complicated nature of science, health, and medicine isn't easily defined; it's full of contradictions. How could a potential poison be good for you at certain doses? Appealing to nature helps us create a simpler world, one in which we can assign causality.

The "Paleo Diet" craze has recently swept through the Western world, indoctrinating people with the dietary concepts of bacon grease, copious amounts of meat, and lightly-cooked vegetables. The idea of "living naturally" often makes reference to our earlier ancestors who supposedly suffered lower levels of disease. This idea often misses one important caveat: early man's lifespan was quite limited. Our ancestors dealt with saber-tooth tigers, injuries, infections, diseases, other people killing them, and a long list of other factors I couldn't even imagine. Early humans simply didn't live long enough to suffer from diseases like cancer, Alzheimer's and osteoporosis.

The natural fallacy operates on an ethical level as well. The appeal to nature extends beyond product marketing into our values. When we experience something as "natural", the conveyed message is that it is intrinsically good. People may think, "If something is natural, it must be morally acceptable because the higher powers have arranged for it to exist." This idea presents some problems. Professor Steven Pinker describes it perfectly, *"The naturalistic fallacy is the idea that what is found in nature is good. It was the basis for Social Darwinism, the belief that helping the poor and sick would get in the way of evolution, which depends on the survival of the fittest. Today, biologists denounce the Naturalistic Fallacy because they want to describe the natural world honestly, without people deriving morals about how we ought to behave. As in: If birds and beasts engage in adultery, infanticide, cannibalism, it must be OK."*[xliv]

The naturalistic fallacy has fueled some of the last century's greatest health hoaxes and convinced millions to play along. For example, take shark cartilage, which was used as a supposedly powerful anti-cancer drug. This craze was based on a 1950's study by John Prudden that said sharks don't get cancer; because of this, millions bought this popular alternative medicine. Only when modern science showed us sharks <u>do</u> regularly get cancer [xlv] did people more-or-less abandon this idea (it's still available for purchase). Or, consider heroin-laced cough syrup. Developed by Bayer Laboratories in 1898, this remedy became all the rage, until it was found to be terribly addictive and discontinued in 1910.

Some natural remedies have continued to this day; take tobacco, for example. Originally called the "holy herb" or "God's remedy", this pervasive little plant has been used for everything from disinfecting, relieving headaches and colds, staving off fatigue, fighting disease, and even pain relief[xlvi]. If that doesn't sound outrageous enough, what about tobacco enemas? These were real treatments in the 17th to 19th centuries. This appeal to good health even resulted in tobacco toothpaste. Imagine that. Crest toothpaste—tobacco flavor. It wasn't until an Indian Supreme Court hearing in 1992[xlvii](yes, 1992) that good old fashioned tobacco toothpaste was banned.

If none of these "natural" remedies have appalled you, the last one will—tapeworms. These became a treatment option for overweight people in the 1950s. They would actually infect themselves with these meter-long parasitic worms in an effort to lose weight. The idea was simple: whatever food you ate would have to be split with the tapeworm. The problem is this: the parasitic worms weren't obedient guests; they often left the

confines of the stomach to travel throughout the body—
even to people's brains.[xlviii]

The above examples are quite shocking. However, if you
ask the people around you, you will certainly find several
examples of this naturalistic fallacy. A certain coworker
of mine has, for the last several months, decided to
purposely ignore the several-hundred-year old practice
of dentistry in favor of "rinsing" his mouth with coconut
oil. He is an otherwise intelligent person, but he has
adopted this idea—and defends it. We are stubborn
creatures; when we decide something is right, there is
often no way to change our minds.   Regardless of
evidence that is only a Google search away, we stick with
simple narratives to help us understand the world and
justify our positions.

The naturalistic fallacy is one of monstrous importance.
When we judge events or options solely on their
"naturalness" or "unnaturalness" we aren't thinking
clearly. The world isn't black-and-white; the best choices
require careful rational analysis. This idea is best
captured by Carl Sagan: *"Deluded or not, supporters of
superstition and pseudoscience are human beings with real
feelings, who, like the skeptics, are trying to figure out how
the world works and what our role in it might be. Their
motives are in many cases consonant with science. If their
culture has not given them all the tools they need to pursue
this great quest, let us temper our criticism with kindness.
None of us comes fully equipped"*.

Chapter 17:
The Middle Ground Fallacy

♦ ♦ ♦

"The problem with our obsession to always see two sides of every issue equally... It means we have to pretend there are always two truths, and the side that doesn't know anything has something to say."

—Bill Maher

If you were willing to sell me your car for ten thousand dollars and I was only willing to pay fifty dollars, compromising and settling at five-thousand wouldn't be a great idea. What if, while discussing whether aliens actually built the pyramids, you came across an argument like this: *"I'm willing to admit that aliens might not have built the pyramids and helped ancient man construct all those monoliths, but you gotta believe that aliens <u>do</u> exist. Isn't that reasonable?"*

When it comes to the truth, there shouldn't be any compromise. When there is, this is called the "middle ground" fallacy. This fallacy has a plethora of names: "argument to moderation", "false compromise", "gray fallacy", "golden means fallacy", and "splitting the difference". The last one, splitting the difference, exemplifies the core problem with this fallacy—agreeing to compromise between two extreme positions. When two sides of an argument are assumed to have equally comparable value, the natural conclusion is that the truth lies in the middle. As you may recall, false dilemmas exist when you must choose only one side of a supposedly two-sided debate which is actually more complicated than "black-and-white". The middle ground fallacy is an inverted false dilemma; you must disregard the extremes and find a middle ground.

Once again, we run into the problem of premises. While both sides of an argument may be extremely opposed, it doesn't mean they're both right. As I said earlier, using unfounded premises to make decisions leads to bad conclusions. Just because there are only two options available in an argument doesn't make them valid; they could both be terribly wrong. The idea that we must endure this balancing act to find a decision is well-ingrained in our culture. Western people strive to make decisions in impartial, unbiased ways. We avoid supporting one side and marginalizing the other. When confronted with controversial issues or decisions that could have social ramifications, we seek balance. If two friends of our friends are arguing, we wouldn't likely walk up and tell them, "You two are both wrong". Most people seek compromises that soften the blow of "being wrong". We are often forced to make a choice: either come across as brutally honest and possibly offensive, or compromise the truth between two unproven and subjective claims.

This belief that both sides of an argument have equal validity tricks us into a mathematical misunderstanding. Remember, we humans aren't particularly good at judging probabilities. When we examine two outcomes or ideas, we often assign a fifty-fifty probability to each. This allocation of probability indicates they must both be considered equally. Faced with a fifty-percent chance of being wrong, we typically opt for the middle option. This is just simple, time-saving math in action. When faced with a problem, we don't bust out a paper and pen and start running regression analyses to determine each variable's relationship. Our brain wants a "quick and dirty" answer—and compromising provides that.

Often, one of these arguments is just a steaming pile of bullshit. No amount of compromise, negotiation, or equivocating can make it true. However, for the sake of political correctness and equality, we often give fringe ideas a chance. Political correctness is vital, and I in no way attempting to tarnish its importance. However, exceptions do exist. When we give fair and equal consideration to ideas that are absolutely ridiculous and highly unscientific, we give them undue credibility.

By even mentioning these ideas in a public forum, we give them a credibility they would not otherwise receive. Take C-SPAN for example; a government-funded network that discusses political issues. Following its mandate of giving equal weight to all sides, C-Span decided to host David Irving, a prominent holocaust denier[xlix]. I think the only reserved spot for a holocaust denier would be somewhere in hell, not on a publically-funded television program.

This act of "balancing the absurd" plays out in many arenas, such as the American school system. Some American States have mandated the teaching of both the theory of evolution and intelligent design. One of these is based on a massive amount of scientifically-valid evidence, the other is not based on any credible scientific evidence. Despite the fact that creationists' claims have been overwhelming discredited by the scientific community, the middle ground fallacy still encourages us to compromise. Political decision-makers should use the best possible evidence and base their choices on the truth. They should not attempt to balance both sides of arguments like these.

In personal arguments, the effects of the middle ground fallacy are often quite innocuous. When it comes to major issues, however, the repercussions can be much more severe. Issues of health and science often suffer from this need for social balance. Despite overwhelming amounts of evidence that clearly show vaccines don't cause autism, media sources still give attention to anti-vaccination groups. By putting people like this into the media spotlight, we validate their claims and give them a public platform to leverage their nonsense. While scientists use statistics, experiments, and rigorously-tested results to corroborate their results, fringe groups often rely only on anecdotal evidence. When we listen to arguments, we must be particularly cautious of those that involve human stories. Anecdotal stories shortcut our rational thinking and make us prone to emotional decision-making. When it comes to decisions that hold the potential for widespread societal change, emotions shouldn't be part of the decision-making process. Emotive stories often resonate much deeper with people, but they don't help us make good decisions.

Never before have humans being inundated with so much information. When faced with the sheer volume of information out there, we must exercise caution. When you consider the amount of information available; you might think about the incredible learning opportunity. While some may use the Internet as a platform to counteract their prejudice and become smarter, the majority of people will simply take whatever crap they find online, absorb it, and transition from having no opinion to having the wrong one. With blogging, YouTubing, and social media, the barriers of entry to share your ideas have become incredibly low. We become overwhelmed and often take sides or stand in an equally-invalid middle ground.

Much of the time the truth does, in fact, lie between two points. However, sometimes both sides of an argument are a lie—or one side is totally wrong. Either way, the halfway point between the truth and a lie is still a lie. As imminent scientist Richard Dawkins said, "*when two opposite points of view are expressed with equal intensity, the truth does not necessarily lie exactly halfway between them. It is possible for one side to be simply wrong.*"

Chapter 18:
Loaded Questions

♦ ♦ ♦

Bob and Steve have been both chasing the same girl, Mary, for quite some time. One weekend, while both are sitting nearby Mary, Bob inquires if Steve has finally kicked his crack cocaine addiction.

In this situation, Steve is forced to explain that he doesn't smoke crack cocaine and that any crack-cocaine smoke allegations are unfounded. Meanwhile, Bob gains the upper hand; albeit, only temporarily. When we ask a question that contains an unjustified or controversial assumption, we commit the "loaded question" fallacy. Loaded questions are designed to confuse listeners into accepting something as true. In order not to appear insensitive, we often give people the benefit of doubt. The person who must reply to an assumption often falls directly into the questioner's agenda. Consider this even more direct example: What if Bob had asked, "Have you stopped smoking crack yet?" Whether Steve answers "yes" or "no", he is admitting his illicit drug consumption. When the facts are presupposed by the question, we become trapped by the limited nature of the possible answers. When we hear a question like this, we are more likely to accept the possibility of the presupposed event.

Loaded questions hoodwink us into an incomplete analysis of an argument. Premises are often left unexamined; the resulting conclusions are weak. Take this, for example. "How many school shootings will we experience before we decide it's time to change gun laws?" When presented with complex social problems, we look for complicated answers. We are subject to two implied claims: that school shootings will occur again, and that gun laws play a significant role. Hearing this loaded question activates our search for an appropriate answer; this acts as a distraction from what we should be doing: rejecting the implicit claim made in the question. We look past the premises to contend with the conclusion.

Loaded questions can come in many shapes and forms. Without constant vigilance, they can slip by our conscious detection and take us places we don't want to be. For example, in a 1996 "60-Minutes interview, interviewer Lesley Stahl slipped a tricky loaded question into her conversation with then Secretary of State, Madeleine Albright. Stahl asked, "*We have heard that half a million children have died. I mean, that is more than died in Hiroshima. And, you know, is the price worth it?* To which, Albright responded, "*I think that is a very hard choice, but the price, we think, the price is worth it*". This was a bad move on Albright's part; by accepting this premise (that it's okay to kill children), she was made to look as if she was justifying the event. Albright later responded by saying, "*I must have been crazy; I should have answered the question by reframing it and pointing out the inherent flaws in the premise behind it.... As soon as I had spoken, I wished for the power to freeze time and take back those words. My reply had been a terrible mistake, hasty, clumsy, and wrong.... I had fallen into a trap and said something that I simply did not mean. That is no one's fault but my own.*[1] The loaded question is a difficult one to avoid, especially when posed during a heated emotional battle.

People utilize the loaded question to engage in an equally cunning method of reasoning—the use of "leading questions". Leading questions supply the answer within the question; the question invokes associations. This is similar to establishing multiple premises within a question; each premise must be refuted to establish truthfulness. In the legal world, these questions in are forbidden. A skilled legal prosecutor can use leading questions to coerce witnesses into answering questions they might otherwise regret. What if I asked, "How fast was the orange car going when it smashed into the red family van?" This question is loaded with assumptions. The orange car was made to look at fault and the word "smash" indicates a high-speed collision. This question is clearly seeking a particular answer: in this case, admitting that the orange car was at fault.

This form of question-asking, although banned from courtroom use, is widely used in journalism. This specific tactic of reporting is called "gotcha media". The goal of gotcha media is to trap interviewees into making damaging statements and careless omissions. These techniques often devolve into direct manipulation via video editing. By taking statements out of context and asking leading and loaded questions, journalists can represent people in whatever light they choose.

What this fallacy shares with the ones I've already discussed is a weak premise. When we make assumptions based on unsound premises, we arrive at bad conclusions. When those premises are already established for us, loaded questions force us to answer within the confines of an independently-decided set of premises. The other person often sets us up to fail. Even by attempting to answer a loaded question, we are in fact, giving it credibility. The next time you encounter a loaded question, stop. Think before you simply react. Otherwise, you might find yourself in a place you don't want to be.

Chapter 19:
The Texas Sharpshooter Fallacy

♦ ♦ ♦

You have probably never heard of the book, Futility. It was an 1897 novel by Morgan Robertson, in which he described the sinking of a massive vessel that bore an uncanny resemblance to the Titanic. Written fourteen years before the Titanic's sinking, Futility describes a huge ship considered unsinkable and adorned with every luxury imaginable. The ship in Futility is named Titan and eventually sinks after striking an iceberg. The Titan's sinking is a disaster; one that is made worse by the limited number of lifeboats. Did "Futility" predicting this disaster? Or was it just a coincidence?

This demonstrates the "Texas sharpshooter fallacy", named after a parable involving a wild Texan shooting his gun indiscriminately at the side of a barn. The Texan walks over to his bullet holes, paints a bull's-eye around them, and proclaims himself a sharpshooter. Although his shots were anything but aimed and accurate, his painting of the bull's-eye makes it appear as if he has performed a highly non-random act. On a normal shooting range, Mr. Texan would suffer from a low probability of hitting the bull's-eye, since the target is already decided and cannot be moved. However, in the Texas sharpshooter fallacy, the region of significance or focus is decided after the event has occurred. This fallacy enables people to make an outcome appear anyway they like. This fallacy uses the same data to both construct and test a hypothesis[li].

The Texas sharpshooter fallacy raises artificial order over natural random chance. When faced with new information, we must choose between two choices: Do we disregard contradictory information in favor of previously-held beliefs, or do we assign newly created meaning to an event to make it support our beliefs? We must choose either to ignore it or reinterpret it. When we choose the latter, we can assign whatever meanings we want by cherry-picking clusters of information to support our arguments—or find a pattern that fits a presumption or stereotype.

We often choose information that supports our motives while disregarding conflicting information. Our chosen similarities become our focus point and we run into a big problem: we see patterns where they don't exist. Our brains are giant pattern recognition systems; we see patterns emerge as the result of interactions between two things. We expand on that pattern and make generalized rules for categorizing future information. This works well in creating "heuristics", those general cognitive "rules of thumb". These provide a framework for making decisions based on recognized patterns. The problem is, sometimes a pattern just doesn't exist—but we create one anyway. If you have a working human brain, you'll almost always try to understand new information when you encounter it. You will think, "What does this event mean?" Remember, you need to assign meaning activates your brain's hyper-active pattern detection system.

When we encounter ambiguous or random information, we often don't discount it as random; instead, we search for meaning. Consider this script by Nostradamus:

Beasts wild with hunger will cross the rivers,
The greater part of the battle will be against Hister.
He will cause great men to be dragged in a cage of iron,
When the son of Germany obeys no law.

Or perhaps, creepier yet.

Out of the deeper part of the west of Europe,
From the poor people a young child shall be born,
Who with his tongue shall seduce many people,
His fame shall increase in the Eastern Kingdom.

This script is from Michel Nostradamus, a 16th century astrologer who wrote four-line verses (quatrains) that supposedly predicted future events. Aside from the fact that the majority of Nostradamus's writings were gibberish and incomprehensible, people throughout the world have assigned meaning to his "prophecies". Consider the above text; it seems shockingly accurate. Upon first encountering the mention of a battle against Hister, we immediately think of Hitler, which fits perfectly into the setting described here. Already, our pattern-detection machines are excited; we feel ourselves closing in on a faulty, but satisfying, decision. As historian and noted skeptic, James Randi, has pointed out, "*Hister is not an ancient name for Hitler, rather, it is for a geographical region near the lower Danube River*". The problem with writings like Nostradamus's is how open they are to interpretation. Just like when you read your horoscope, any vague information can be bent and manipulated to fit any meaning or purpose. Random events are only meaningful after we decide they are. Often, these decisions are not based on reality—but on wishful thinking.

This effect is referred to as the "Forer Effect", based on the observation that individuals will give high accuracy ratings to descriptions they believe are custom-tailored to them. These descriptions are often so vague and meaningless that they could apply to a wide range of people. The term was coined after psychologist, Betram R. Forer, gave a psychology test to a group of his students, who were told they would each receive a brief vignette or sketch of their personality. Upon receiving the sketch of their personality, they were asked to rate it, and decide how much it applied to them. In reality, each student received the exact same sketch, including these items (among others):

- You have a great need for other people to like and admire you.
- Disciplined and self-controlled outside, you tend to be worrisome and insecure inside.
- You have a great deal of unused capacity which you have not turned to your advantage.
- At times, you are extroverted, affable, sociable, while at other times you are introverted, wary, and reserved.
- You pride yourself as an independent thinker and do not accept others' statements without satisfactory proof.

Forer's students, on average, rated the accuracy of these statements as 4.26 out of 5. They are so general they can apply to everyone; however, by assigning individual meanings to each, they suddenly become much more consequential.

When we seek meaning, we want things to "line up"; we ignore the noise of conflicting information. When we find meaning, we overlook the "chance factor" and the randomness of our experience to assign things with lasting importance and value. In retrospect, our brains work like a video editor. We take hundreds of hours of footage, cut it up into little bits, delete a few scenes, and finalize the end product – one that depicts a certain story or event while ignoring everything else. We create a narrative and meaning out of the chaos of life.

Despite the fact that this fallacy has a unique and amusing name, it's the core reason why scientists form hypotheses and then try to disprove them. They want to avoid making this mistake. Epidemiologists are especially cautious of the Texas sharpshooter fallacy; they want to know what factors truly affect the spread of disease—not to focus on only one possibility.

For example, if you were to plot all the areas in the US where cancer rates are the highest, you would identify certain areas with a "clumping" of data. You could assume these areas contained toxic dump sites, power lines, high concentrations of airborne chemicals, or even old nuclear test sites. The problem is, cancer is a tricky bastard—if you try to identify the cause of a cluster of cancer cases on a map, you become vulnerable to the sharpshooter fallacy.

In a 1999 New Yorker article, "The Cancer Cluster Myth", an expert said, *"A community that is afflicted with an unusual number of cancers quite naturally looks for a cause in the environment—in the ground, the water, the air. And the correlations are sometimes found: the cluster may arise after, say, contamination of the water supply by a possible carcinogen. The problem is that when scientists have tried to confirm such causes, they haven't been able to. Raymond Richard Neutra, California's chief environmental health investigator and an expert on cancer clusters, points out that among hundreds of exhaustive, published investigations of residential clusters in the United States, not one has convincingly identified an underlying environmental cause. Abroad, in only a handful of cases has a neighborhood cancer cluster been shown to arise from an environmental cause. And only one of these cases ended with the discovery of an unrecognized carcinogen."[lii]* We aren't able to specifically identify which factors contribute to higher cancer rates; any attempt to do so is merely an exercise in assigning causality—whether valid or invalid.

Life is chaotic; sometimes we can find no meaning to the countless ironies, tragedies, and injustices we encounter. When we see the world in this way, we experience a deep sense of anxiety; we are unable to come to terms with the randomness and seemingly cruelness of the world. This powerlessness—this feeling of being absolutely defenseless against chance and randomness—can be ameliorated by singling out an antagonist. By focusing on one agent of cause, we can understand an event and assign blame. We crave the "bad guy", the culprit, the "evil menace" who makes our world easier to understand. This need to make our worlds easier to understand is a fallacy called the "just-world hypothesis". This hypothesis describes our tendency to attribute consequences to—or expect consequences as a result of—a universal force that restores moral balance. In the end, all evil actions are punished and all good ones are rewarded. We may call this "cosmic justice", "order", "stability", or any number of other misnomers; however, the end goal is still the same— understanding this crazy world. Even when there is no blame to assign, we often "cherry-pick" our data and identify real or imaginary culprits.

One of the most poignant examples of our ability to make

randomness meaningful comes in the form of a piece of toast. A woman who claimed a ten-year-old grilled cheese sandwich bore the image of the Virgin Mary sold a couple of pieces of white bread and a slice of processed cheese for $28,000 on eBay[liii]. She said this sandwich was special because it didn't sprout any mold, despite sitting on her bedside table for several years. This ridiculous (and perhaps slightly over-the-top) example keenly demonstrates our ability to "cherry-pick" the information we like best from a story.

Sometimes, though, a pattern seems legitimate. During World War II, Londoners noticed that German bombing raids consistently missed certain neighborhoods. These perceived patterns of <u>targeted</u> bombings led people to suspect these buildings had been spared intentionally. People eventually began to believe that these "special buildings" were occupied by German spies[liv]. However, a later comprehensive survey of bombing strike patterns by Amos Tversky and Daniel Kahneman showed them to be random. Londoners confronted with the utter mayhem of the bombings were in desperate need to find meaning in this chaos. Why were some people's homes still standing while others' were terribly destroyed? When we face the randomness of events, we seek a "just world"—one that allows us to make sense of things.

We don't want to admit we're wrong; we definitely don't want to admit how messy, chaotic and random life is. We are fairly helpless; some causal events are so complicated we can never know the why they happened. We rarely reflect on our inabilities to truly understand the "how's and whys" behind the events of our lives. It can be painful to admit that random chance rules your life. When we face this dilemma, the Texas sharpshooter fallacy offers us a way out—a way to provide meaning, assign blame, and make excuses.

We fear the uncertainty of "not knowing" to a great degree. Seeking order is a primal need; we need a simple path to follow while navigating this crazy existence. We seek this order through patterns—patterns we can rely on to help us interpret events. Whether a pattern is real or imagined, it still fulfills the same goal—creating a world we can understand.

Chapter 20:
Our Self-Made Worlds

◆ ◆ ◆

"A world that can be explained, even with bad reasons, is a familiar world. But, on the other hand, in a universe suddenly divested of illusions and lights, man feels an alien, a stranger. His exile is without remedy since he is deprived of the memory of a lost home or the hope of a promised land. This divorce between man and his life, the actor and his setting, is properly the feeling of absurdity."

—Albert Camus

Whether we want to admit it or not, we build and modify our realities every day. We don't experience events without filtering them through our experiences, emotions, and ideas. One person may experience an event entirely differently than another. An "objective reality" <u>does</u> exist, but we rarely consider it. For the most part, we exist in a subjective-social world, one in which we create, modify, and manipulate meanings to serve our purposes. Life appears before our eyes and we interpret it the best we can. Most of what we experience contains

122

no intrinsic meaning; we <u>ascribe</u> meaning to events by assuming, projecting, and wishing.

We engage in actions that otherwise rational minds would reject. In Jonathan Heidt's epic book,[iv] *The Righteous Mind*, he says, "The human mind is a story processor, not a logic processor". Our journey together in his book—through the landscape of logical fallacies and biases—underlines the poignancy of this idea. We often act without logic in order to maintain the safety of our "narratives". Earlier, I mentioned Dan Sperber's "argumentative theory of reasoning", in which he claims, "The *argumentative theory of reasoning – proposes that instead of having a purely individual function, reasoning has a social and, more specifically, argumentative function.*"[lvi] Sperber argues that rational thinking and reasoning appeared not out of a need to find the truth, but rather as a defensive mechanism – one designed to protect our story.

Our insistence on appearing certain and correct is essential to our maintenance of valid personal narratives. Like watching clouds form and take shapes, we create a fiction from the parts and pieces of our lives. We string these bits together and solidify them into personal narratives. Any attack on (or perceived threat to) our narratives threatens to break these "strings".

Our personal narratives include our value systems and self-image; we build these carefully, but only superficially examine them. We use our values and opinions as a metric for evaluating (and engaging with) the world. To maintain the stability we require to have a "strong ego", our minds have built-in cognitive devices that maintain our narratives and reject any pieces of conflicting information. These "protection devices" are the cognitive biases or heuristics that our brains use to streamline incoming information. We are not open to all information; rather, only information that fits our beliefs. Cognitive biases serve an important evolutionary role – to simplify our existence.

Life is a chaotic mess. We need consistency—we crave it. Our routines provide consistency, stability, and reassurance; they are our fortresses of security and comfort. We know what's going on inside of us and resist outward change. Routines can also develop in our minds; these appear as our resistance to contradiction and challenge. However, the consistency we seek in our lives by creating narratives is <u>best</u> exemplified by our need to <u>be right</u>. However, don't be fooled—our need to be right doesn't always serve an "egotistical" agenda of proving others wrong; it also serves to destroy contradictions and protect ourselves.

To protect our self-image, ideas, and opinions, we deploy faulty reasoning and logical fallacies; these fallacies ensure our arguments' victory and render our opponents' arguments ineffectual. We can create and support any ideas in our minds; our powers of self-delusion are phenomenal. This can be a lifelong issue; many of us go to our deathbeds with our illusions still clutched tightly in our hands.

However, we <u>can</u> find a way out. This path was first explored by the Ancient Greeks, who venerated rational discourse and logic above all other things. The Greek love for rhetoric was a sword that cut through the restrictions of self-delusion. Questioning the "why" behind all things is the essence of a good rhetorician. By reading this book, you have effectively completed a course in rhetoric. Examining your thoughts is the first step in living a better life; you will make better decisions, escape self-delusion, and liberate yourself from the need to always be right.

"Your pain is the breaking of the shell that encloses your understanding."

—Khalil Gibran 1883-1931

Conclusion

Dear Reader,

If you've stayed with me until the end of this book, I greatly appreciate your support. I undertook this project for two reasons: to better understand myself and to share my knowledge with others. As a self-published author, I don't get the same media attention, editorial reviews, and marketing assistance as authors who work with major publishers. My readers' opinions mean the world to me and I would be incredibly appreciative of your feedback.

If you have a few extra minutes, please leave a review and share your thoughts.

I greatly appreciate you reading this book and your interest in my work is extremely important to me.

On my personal website, I research and write weekly articles about business, life and personal development. The question that I strive to ask is, "How can I improve my life every day".

If science-based self-improvement is something you are interested in, please sign up to my weekly newsletter – where I will send you free books and articles. (Sign up by clicking on this text.)

If weekly emails bother you or you simply aren't interested, no problem – please don't sign up.

I still like you for reading this book and hope you enjoyed it.

Sia M.

Other books by Sia Mohajer:

The Little Book of Stupidity: How We Lie to Ourselves and Don't Believe Others

"As human beings, we are great story tellers. We tell stories about who we are, what we're doing, and why we do it. The problem is, sometimes these stories are fictions created by our own blindness to reality. We are such good story tellers that we often don't know we're deceiving ourselves. Our brains have evolved to process information simply; however, this creates a need in us to simplify the world. Sometimes, we sacrifice our rational thinking to achieve this simplicity. In The Little Book of Stupidity, Sia Mohajer draws on extensive research and makes surprising connections between 10 of Life's Most Pervasive Cognitive Biases. This book is a story about how stupid we can all be—and how we can become more compassionate as a result of this awareness."

The Little Book of Persuasion: Defend Yourself and Become a Skilled Persuader

"Every day, we engage in psychological battles to persuade others—or be persuaded by them. The history of persuasion dates back to the Ancient Greeks, who valued rhetoric as an essential skill. However, times have changed; rhetoric has lost its place in culture as a fundamental skill of reasoning and logic. Our ignorance of rhetoric leaves us open and unarmed—and vulnerable to skilled persuaders.

Persuasion is about a lot more than just tactics and methods of social compliance. Understanding how we are persuaded opens the doorway to a deeper understanding of our automatic brain processes and biases. Expert persuaders tap into these processes and use them against us for their own benefit. This book guides you through the journey of discovering and developing these rhetorical techniques. You will emerge from this process smarter, more persuasive, and better equipped to defend yourself."

Footnotes

i https://en.wikipedia.org/wiki/Ulric_Neisser

ii http://dangerousintersection.org/2008/10/12/what-it-means-to-feel-certain-review-of-on-being-certain/

iii https://en.wikipedia.org/wiki/List_of_cognitive_biases

iv http://blogs.discovermagazine.com/intersection/2011/04/25/is-reasoning-built-for-winning-arguments-rather-than-finding-truth/#.VmQxG3arRD8

v https://en.wikipedia.org/wiki/Cognitive_bias

vi http://www.fbi.gov/about-us/cjis/ucr/crime-in-the-u.s/2010/crime-in-the-u.s.-2010/offenses-known-to-law-enforcement/expanded/expandhomicidemain

vii http://arstechnica.com/science/2011/04/guns-in-the-home-lots-of-risk-ambiguity/

viii http://blogs.scientificamerican.com/cross-check/did-the-u-s-overreact-to-the-911-attacks-undoubtedly/

ix http://www.psmag.com/health-and-behavior/confident-idiots-92793

x http://www.psmag.com/health-and-behavior/confident-idiots-92793

xi Morris, Errol (20 June 2010). "The Anosognosic's Dilemma: Something's Wrong but You'll Never Know What It Is (Part 1)". *New York Times.* Retrieved 7 March 201

xii http://www.nature.com/mp/journal/v6/n5/full/4000918a.html

xiii 5https://en.wikipedia.org/wiki/Mesolimbic_pathway

xiv 6http://www.columbiapsych.com/shame_miller.html

xv 7https://en.wikipedia.org/wiki/Reason#Classical_philosophy

xvi 8https://books.google.com.tw/books?id=oMNUBAAAQBA

xvii https://en.wikipedia.org/wiki/Three_Mile_Island_accident

xviii 10 Agassi, Joseph (2008). "Rationality and the *tu quoque* argument". *Inquiry* **16** (1–4): 395–406

xix 10 http://www.policymic.com/articles/4095/bank-bailouts-why-barack-obama-very-much-is-a-socialist

11 http://rationalwiki.org/wiki/Gish_Gallop

xx http://rationalwiki.org/wiki/Peanut_butter_argument

xxi 11 http://rationalwiki.org/wiki/Russell%27s_Teapot

xxii 13 http://rationalwiki.org/wiki/Lawrence_v._Texas

xxiii 12 http://usatoday30.usatoday.com/news/washington/2003-04-23-santorum-excerpt_x.htm

xxiv 14 http://mentalfloss.com/article/53330/17-bizarre-natural-remedies-1700s

xxv 16 http://rationalwiki.org/wiki/Welfare_queen

xxvi 15 Gibson, Rhonda; Zillman, Dolf (1994). "Exaggerated Versus Representative Exemplification in News Reports: Perception of Issues and Personal Consequences". *Communication Research* **21** (5): 603–624.

xxvii Jenicek, M. (1999). *Clinical Case Reporting in Evidence-Based Medicine.* Oxford: Butterworth–Heinemann. p. 117.

xxvii http://skepdic.com/testimon.html

xxviii http://skepdic.com/testimon.html

xxix http://xkcd.com/552/

xxx 17 http://rationalwiki.org/wiki/Post_hoc,_ergo_propter_hoc

xxxi http://www.logicallyfallacious.com/index.php/logical-fallacies/29-appeal-to-emotion

xxxii 18 Seneca, De Ira, 1, viii

xxxiii 19 Aristotle, Rhetorica 1

xxxiv 19 Edward Bernays, Propaganda, 1928, 2005 ed., p.72

xxxv 20 Dan Ariely, "The Irrational Bundle." iBooks. Dan Ariely. "The Irrational Bundle.", p.764

xxxvi Robin L. Nabi, "Discrete Emotions and Persuasion," in "Persuasion and the Structure of Affect", The Persuasion Handbook, Sage Publishing, p.296

xxxvii 22Meany 2002, p. 65.

xxxviii 23Meany 2002, p. 65.

xxxix 23 www.wikipedia.com/steven_fry

xl R. H. Robbins, "Browne, Sir Thomas (1605–1682)", *Oxford Dictionary of National Biography*, Oxford University Press, 2004; online edn, May 2008 xli http://www.txstate.edu/philosophy/resources/fallacy-definitions/Begging-the-Question.html

xlii http://skepdic.com/begging.html

xliii http://skepdic.com/begging.html

xliv http://thedailyomnivore.net/2012/11/05/naturalistic-fallacy/

xlv http://www.abc.net.au/science/articles/2005/09/08/1410188.htm

xlvi
http://www.scienceandsociety.co.uk/results.asp?image=10328187&screenwidth=721

xlvii http://www.ncbi.nlm.nih.gov/pmc/articles/PMC1759563/

xlviii https://www.sciencebasedmedicine.org/worms-germs-and-dirt-what-can-they-teach-us-about-allergies-and-autoimmune-diseases/

xlix http://www.washingtonpost.com/wp-dyn/articles/A35346-2005Mar14.html

l Albright, Madeleine (2003). *Madam Secretary: A Memoir*. p. 275. ISBN 0-7868-6843-0.

li http://rationalwiki.org/wiki/Texas_sharpshooter_fallacy

lii http://www.newyorker.com/magazine/1999/02/08/the-cancer-cluster-myth

liii http://www.nbcnews.com/id/6511148/ns/us_news-weird_news/t/virgin-mary-grilled-cheese-sells/#.VlKhj3arRD8

liv http://merrynallingham.com/spies-and-suspicions-on-the-home-front/?doing_wp_cron=1448293499.5448150634765625000000

lv
https://books.google.com.tw/books?id=U21BxGfm3RUC&printsec=frontcover&hl=en#v=onepage&q=%22human%20mind%20is%20a%20story%20processor%2C%20not%20a%20logic%20processor%22&f=false

lvi
https://sites.google.com/site/hugomercier/theargumentativetheoryofreasoning

Made in the USA
Columbia, SC
07 September 2018